SABRE & LANCE

PETER NEWARK

SABRE & LANCE

AN ILLUSTRATED HISTORY OF CAVALRY

BLANDFORD PRESS

POOLE · NEW YORK · SYDNEY

FOR OLLIE
WHO HELPED ME

First published in the UK 1987 by Blandford Press
Link House, West Street, Poole, Dorset BH15 1LL

Copyright © 1987 Peter Newark

Distributed in the United States by
Sterling Publishing Co. Inc,
2 Park Avenue, New York, NY 10016

Distributed in Australia by
Capricorn Link (Australia) Pty Ltd
PO Box 665, Lane Cove, NSW 2066

British Library Cataloguing in Publication Data

Newark, Peter
  Sabre and lance : an illustrated history
  of cavalry.
  1. Cavalry— History
  I. Title
  357'.1'09   UE15

ISBN 0 7137 1813 7

Typeset by Best-set Typesetter Hong Kong
Printed in Yugoslavia

CONTENTS

ACKNOWLEDGEMENTS

The illustrations, of which a large number have been only rarely reproduced in the past, are mostly from my own extensive collection of military prints and paintings, and I hereby acknowledge the hard work undertaken by my wife Ollie in researching and collating the pictures for this book.

I also wish to thank in particular the following people who have helped me with information and illustrations: Lt Colonel R.B. Anderson, OBE, The Royal Scots Dragoon Guards (Carabiniers & Greys); Lt Colonel R.L.C. Tamplin, Regimental Secretary, the 17th/21st Lancers; Lt Colonel J.E. Roderick, Canadian Defense Liaison Staff (London); Lt Colonel R.B. Merton, Regimental Secretary, The Royal Hussars (PWO); Lt Colonel A.D. Meakin, Curator, Household Cavalry Museum; R. Thompson, Museum of 15th/19th The King's Royal Hussars; Roy Butler of The Military Heritage Museum, Lewes, Sussex; Victor J.H. Suthren of the Canadian War Museum, Ottawa, Ontario; Nicholas Wilkey of Military Matters, Bath.

I also acknowledge the work of the authors of the many books I have consulted and drawn from and a selective bibliography will be found at the end of this volume.

Peter Newark
Bath, England, 1986

PREFACE

This book presents a cavalcade of cavalry from ancient to modern times. It traces the development and deployment of horse soldiers of the major military powers, with an introductory chapter by Tim Newark, an authority on ancient and medieval warfare.

At one time, it had been considered to use for the title of this book the regimental motto of the 17th Prussian Hussars 'Death or Glory'. This is also the motto of Britain's 17th/21st Lancers, whose badge is the 'Death's Head' with the motto 'Or Glory.' These three words, when coupled the names of the horse soldier's weapons 'Sabre and Lance', seem entirely appropriate in describing such a colourful and dramatic subject: the dash and drive of a cavalry charge.

1 · HORSE WARRIORS

An Introductory Chapter by Tim Newark

At the siege of Rome in AD 537, Belisarius decided to break the deadlock and carry the fighting against the besieging Ostrogoths. With the arrival of 1,600 reinforcements, mostly Avar and Slav horsemen, the Byzantine commander ordered a mounted raid against the Germanic Barbarians. Two hundred warriors were instructed to ride towards the Ostrogoth camp. As soon as they were within sight of the enemy, they were to ascend a nearby hill and wait there. When the Barbarians reacted to this provocation, the Byzantine raiders were not to close in hand to hand combat, but to keep their distance and rake the enemy with their bows and arrows. As soon as their quivers were empty, the Byzantines were then to dash back to the safety of the city before the Germans could catch them. Later that day, Byzantine horsemen burst from the gates of Rome and carried out the raid as ordered. Their arrows felled many of the outraged German horsemen and they were hotly pursued back to their fortifications. On the battlements, Byzantine artillerymen covered their comrades with *ballistae* bolts and the frustrated Barbarians were forced to back away. They had lost many warriors to the Byzantine horse archers.

So successful were these tactics, Belisarius ordered two more similar raids. Equally devastating, the Ostrogoth chieftain replied with like provocation. He sent out his leading warriors with their retinues of horsemen and forced the Byzantines to meet them. But the Byzantine horse archers simply rode around the Germans shooting their bows, weakening them for a final clash in close combat. The Ostrogoths were baffled by these repeated defeats, but the lesson of their conflict was clear to Procopius, the Byzantine eye-witness of the events. 'Almost all the Byzantines and their allies – the Avars – are good mounted bowmen,' he wrote, 'but not a man among the Ostrogoths is practised in this skill because all their horsemen are accustomed to use only spears and swords. Their archers enter battle on foot and under cover of more heavily armed warriors. Therefore, unless the fighting is at close quarters, the German horsemen cannot defend themselves against mounted archers. As for their foot archers, they can never be strong enough to confront men on horseback.'

This fundamental difference between Germanic and Byzantine horse warriors again struck Procopius at the battle of Taginae in 552. In this combat, high in the Apennines, Byzantine archers formed the tips of a crescent into which the Ostrogoth nobles and their horse warriors

galloped. The Byzantines pelted the Germans with a deadly rain of arrows and the Goths, powerless to respond, rode ineffectually on to the Byzantine spearmen. On this occasion, Procopius explained the lack of archers among the Goth horsemen by writing that their leader, in a fit of Germanic folly, had decreed that his warriors should not use bows or any other weapon except their spears. But it is difficult to believe that warriors fighting for their lives would obey such a rash conceit. Procopius was right the first time: Germanic horsemen were accustomed only to fighting with spears and swords, not bows. Such a development among Germanic horse warriors is crucial to an understanding of the entire history of cavalry in Western Europe and why they were so different to Oriental horsemen.

In the ancient and medieval worlds, up until the introduction of effective firearms, the most powerful portable missile weapon was the bow and arrow, especially the Oriental composite bow. And when shot from horseback, it proved an overwhelming military force: combining supreme striking power with mobility. The Romans realised this and employed great numbers of horse archers throughout their Empire. Remains of the composite bows of Oriental auxiliaries have been found as far from their homeland as the fortress of Caerleon in Wales. After the break-up of the Roman Empire, however, and the gradual Germanisation of Europe, horse archers ceased to be a vital or common factor in Western armies. The Germanic reluctance to use bows in the saddle, as described by Procopius, prevailed. And because it was a Germanic martial elite who were to rule

Cavalry skirmish between Russians and Bulgarians in the 10th century. Eastern European warfare continued to be dominated by horsemen and particularly horse archers throughout the Middle Ages. From a Byzantine manuscript in the Vatican Library.

the estates of Europe for centuries, so their military culture determined all
that followed. Thus, medieval knights, the descendants of those aristocratic
Goth horse warriors, never used bows in battle, preferring to rely on their
swords and lances. Western military culture rarely admitted the usefulness
of mounted archers. Even when confronted by Arabs in Spain, Turks in the
Holy Land, or Magyars and Mongols in central Europe, Western knights
never considered adopting the bows of their opponents. Why should
generations of professional warriors neglect a self-evidently useful and
powerful weapon? Only a fool or a saint declines to use arms and tactics
fully employed by his enemies. The majority of European knights were
neither of these.

The answer to this conundrum has been sought in two areas: the first
technical, the second cultural. The composite bow was the most powerful
of bows. It outdistanced all wooden bows, including the so-called longbow.
Its power derived from the combined strength of several materials: a
wooden core was backed with layers of sinew and on the inside with
strips of horn. All these materials were then sandwiched together with
animal glue. The combination of wood, sinew, and horn produced a highly
flexible bow which allowed a far longer draw than was possible from a
wooden bow. But because of its composition of glued materials, one
authority has suggested that the bow was vulnerable to the wet climate of
Europe and for that reason was never adopted in the West. That is untrue:
Asia has its own extremes of climate and elaborate cases were designed to
protect the bow. Besides, the composite bow was used throughout Europe
by mercenary oriental troops. It was also employed extensively in Eastern
Europe by Poles, Hungarians, and Russians.

Another suggested reason for the lack of composite bows in the West is
that there were no long-horn cattle or goats in Europe from which suitable
horn could be obtained. Again, this is untrue. Gilles de Bouvier in the 15th
century describes the warriors of northern Germany as 'good crossbowmen
on foot or horseback, drawing bows of horn and sinew which are good,
accurate and strong because they never snap'. As for the Hungarians. 'They
make serious war on the Saracens and have short bows of horn and sinew

with cranks with which they shoot.' The European crossbow
was the Western version of the composite bow. Much under-
rated by English historians, because of a prejudice against
its use in French armies, the composite crossbow was more
powerful and had a longer range than most Western wooden
bows. There were reflexed wooden bows available in continental Europe as well, using design to compensate for the efficient
materials of the composite bow and crossbow.

The mystery remains: if climate and composition did not
preclude the use of the composite bow in the West, and there
were other effective bows available for use from horseback, why did the knights of Western Europe never add
it to their armoury? Elsewhere, throughout the Eurasian

13

Royal Hunt demonstrating the skill of Persian horse archers. Detail from a Persian manuscript of around 1450.

and Oriental world, the élite professional warriors of every society considered it a necessity and virtue to be highly skilled in horse archery. Finely embellished bows were prized status symbols among these noble warriors. Oriental leaders gave each other gilded bows as a sign of authority. In the West, there were no decorated bows. The solution to this problem lies in the field of Western social and military culture.

'Cursed be the first man who became an archer. He was afraid and did not dare approach.' So wrote Bertrand de Bar-sur-Aube, a poet of the 13th

14

Norman archer pursuing fleeing Saxons at the battle of Hastings, 1066. He is the only mounted archer depicted on the Bayeux Tapestry and may represent a footsoldier simply assuming horse-back to join in the rout, rather than a true horse archer.

century. Throughout the Middle Ages, noble Germanic warriors and knights believed it unmanly and beneath their dignity to kill a warrior from afar with a bow and arrow. True chivalric celebrity was obtained through killing one's enemy in hand to hand combat with lance, sword, or mace. Use of the bow and arrow was left to social inferiors who could not be expected to fight as bravely or daringly as their overlords. And because bows became a regular weapon of socially inferior footsoldiers, so this reinforced knightly prejudice against it. Even when West met East on the plains of central Europe or along the coasts of the Holy Land, Western knights still refused to confront Oriental horse archers on equal terms. The principle of a fair fight – a balanced test of arms – did not extend to a knight equipping himself with a bow. It was the Infidel who was transgressing the laws of manly combat, so why should a knight sink to his level? Retaliatory archery was left to accompanying crowds of underlings and if these proved unable to match the mobility and excellence of mounted Saracen archers, then that was the way it would be. Defeat with dignity, rather than victory through ignoble means.

Illogical and foolish though this may sound, the fact remains that knights never used bows in battle. Of course, they realised the power of the bow.

15

There were schemes to prohibit it from the battlefield. Aristocrats managed to convince the Lateran Council in 1139 of the necessity to ban the use of the crossbow and archery generally against Christians. A decade later, the sanction was promulgated throughout the Holy Roman Empire by Conrad III. In a Lateran Council of 1215, crossbowmen along with mercenary leaders and surgeons were condemned as the most terrible types of men of blood. These prohibitions had little practical effect on the use of archers in the battlefield, but it fixed in the minds of the professional martial élite the prejudice that the bow was not a weapon fit for a man of honour.

Fortunately, the majority of Western knights in their myriad wars were confronted by warriors armed much like themselves. But for those warlords on the eastern borderlands of Europe who realised the necessity of mounted archers, there were means of getting around their chivalric prejudice. From the 12th century onwards, in the Holy Land and gradually throughout the Mediterranean, Saracen horse archers were hired. These mercenaries were called Turcopoles and Frederick II employed many in his Italian campaigns. Beyond the Mediterranean, the powerful skills of native bowmen and crossbowmen became patently clear by the late Middle Ages, so that archers mounted on horseback were a sizeable contingent in most Western armies. On the whole, however, they did not shoot from the saddle. They dismounted as soon as they reached the battlefield. Their horses provided mobility while marching and enabled them to pursue a routed enemy, but no one expected them to incorporate the horse in battle in the manner of the Infidels. Therefore, despite the occasional hiring of Saracen archers, it can be seen that the general prejudice of the knightly class against horse archery dictated tactics even to their social inferiors who certainly had no need to invest in chivalric convention. Because of the lack of interest in bows shown by knights, it meant that the skill of horse archery in the West never achieved the heights of perfection it did among Oriental horsemen. It also deprived Western armies totally of the impact of heavy horse archers, warriors clad in full armour using the bow and then closing with lance and sword.

The few recorded exceptions to this rule of Western medieval warfare tend to reinforce the view that it was ignoble for a professional horse

The King of France unhorsed at the battle of Bouvines, 1214. Rare contemporary illustration of a western medieval horse archer. Drawing by Matthew Paris from his *Historia Majora*, now at Corpus Christi College, Cambridge.

warrior, aspiring to the knightly class, to carry a bow. In his 6th century Frank chronicle, Gregory of Tours mentions a Count Leudast who wore a quiver round his mail shirt. In all other respects, the Count was patently a member of the Frank warrior élite: he wore a helmet, mail, and no doubt rode a horse. Yet he also carried a bow. Perhaps this detail was intended to show that he was a parvenu: he had risen quickly from cook to stable-master to Count and so did not possess the decorum of truly noble warriors. But above all, Leudast had committed crimes against the Church and Gregory. He accused the chronicler of slandering the Queen, by spreading rumours that she was having an affair with a bishop. Gregory got his own back by detailing Leudast's bow-carrying. This transgression of the

Frankish kings Louis and Carloman defeating the Vikings. Another unusual representation of a western medieval horse archer. The artist, Jean Fouquet, may be representing an earlier type of warfare, but the costumes are contemporary and with most medieval illustrations we must assume the artist is illustrating the warfare of his own time and the occurrence of horse archers in 15th century battles. From the *Grandes Chroniques de France*, now in the Bibliothèque Nationale, Paris.

Germanic military code would have been readily noted by an aristocratic reader and automatically cast the Count as a bad sort.

Other evidence of horse warriors who did not always play the game occur in a drawing in the margin of Matthew Paris's 13th century *Historia Majora* (Corpus Christi College, Cambridge, MS 16, f.37). Illustrating the King of France unhorsed at the battle of Bouvines in 1214, it also shows a French knight shooting arrows at the retreating Hugo de Boves. The incident this aspect of the drawing depicts is described in Paris's rendition of Roger of Wendover's chronicle: '*At hostes propius accedere metuentes, lanceis sub ipso tres equos peremerunt.*' Translated, this reads: 'Hugo de Boves' enemies, fearing to come too near him, killed three horses under him with their lances.' Of course, this recorded incident may never have happened: it may be just a made-up heroic image. However, if it is based upon a true event reported from battle, then what is clear is that Hugo's horses were not killed in close combat but presumably by lances thrown overarm in the manner of the Norman warriors depicted on the Bayeux tapestry. Matthew Paris though, in his marginal drawing, has chosen to interpret '*lanceis*' more loosely, meaning not to pierce with a lance, but to launch or project a weapon, in this case an arrow from a bow.

Elsewhere in drawings ascribed to Paris, he is very precise and perceptive

Alexander the Great defeats Darius at the battle of Issus, 333 BC. Alexander came from the horse-breeding region of northern Greece and placed great emphasis on cavalry in his campaigns. Details from a mosaic at Pompeii. Alexander is shown on the left.

18

in his depiction of military equipment and weapons. In the same Cambridge manuscript, he draws a sea-battle in which pots of 'Greek Fire' or another noxious substance are launched from a bow and a sling. Therefore, his rendition of a mounted knight shooting a bow may have some basis in fact. That it was a rare occurrence nevertheless, is demonstrated by the fact that in all other drawings of archers they are shown as common footsoldiers, while mail-clad knights kill each other with lance and sword only. More likely on this occasion, Paris portrayed a knight with a bow to emphasise the cowardliness of Hugo's adversaries. In which case, medieval accounts of knightly mounted archers are largely a literary and artistic device, symbolic of the ignoble and cowardly, rather than being a battlefield reality.

In the early Middle Ages, however, a definite attempt was made by the Carolingians to revive the Roman practice of horse archery. This is indicated by several Carolingian manuscripts. In a letter to the Abbot Fulrad, the Emperor Charlemagne instructed the holy man to supply his army with horsemen equipped specifically with shield, lance, sword, dagger, and bow and arrows. Elsewhere, in a manuscript of 803, each landlord is asked to equip their warriors with a lance, shield, a bow and two bowstrings plus 12 arrows. In this *Capitulare Aquisgranense*, there is a following sentence which states that two men are required to have these weapons between them. This may suggest that a mounted warrior was expected to carry lance and shield, while a dismounted man (a squire in later terms) used the bow. This would certainly fit the status of weapons common in Western Europe. But the summons to Abbot Fulrad does not make this distinction and some military historians have proposed that Charlemagne armed his cavalry with bows especially to counter the Oriental horse archers of the Avars, at that time ravaging central Europe. Such a spur did not convince later warlords, however, and it may have been more directly inspired by old Roman military manuals as part of the general renaissance of Roman culture pursued by the court of Charlemagne.

Bronze statue of a Greek horse warrior of the 6th century BC. Greek horsemen put their fighting faith in javelins thrown at the enemy and swords swung in close combat. Now in the British Museum.

Firmer evidence of Carolingian horse archers is provided by an illustration in the 9th century *Golden Psalter* of St Gall (St Gall, Stiftsbibliothek, Cod.22 p.141). Amid a gang of spear-carrying Carolingian horsemen assaulting a town is a lone heavily armoured horse warrior, in characteristic mail and quasiclassical helmet, drawing a bow.

Beyond the field of battle, according to later medieval manuscripts, horse archery appears to have been acceptable among the noblest warriors only in the pursuit of hunting. In *Queen Mary's Psalter* in the British Museum, possibly made for Edward I or II, there is a marginal detail showing a king shooting a grotesque creature from horseback. He turns in his saddle and shoots backwards. Another picture in the *Decretals of Gregory* (BM Royal MS 10 E iv) shows a king pursuing and shooting a stag with a bow from horseback. It is probably true that such archery may have been acceptable in the chase, when killing animals, but this was a world apart from battle when killing men of equal stature. It is possible, however, that both these details were based on figures adapted from oriental manuscripts as curious artistic motifs.

Drawing of an auxiliary Roman horseman trampling down a barbarian. The Romans employed great numbers of mercenary cavalry, especially Celts and Germans. Many details have now been lost on the original gravestone.

The origin of the aristocratic Germanic prejudice against mounted archery can be traced to Celtic horsemanship and this in turn was influenced by Greek warfare. In a play written by Euripides in the 5th century BC, one of the characters denigrates Heracles' martial prowess: 'he never carried a shield or wielded a spear. He used a bow, the coward's weapon – handy to run away. Bows prove no heroes. The real man is he who stands solid in the ranks and dares to face the thrust of the spear.' Heracles' father replies in his defence: 'The man skilled in archery can maintain a hail of arrows and yet still have some in reserve. He can keep his distance, so that the enemy never see him, only feel his arrows. He never has to expose himself to the enemy. This is the first rule of war – to harm your enemy as long as he stays in range, but always to keep yourself protected.' Despite the good sense of this argument and constant contact with the highly effective horse archers of the Scythians and the Persians,

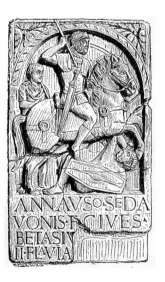

20

Norman knights at the battle of Hastings. They hurl their lances or javelins in a fashion that remained popular in medieval warfare until chivalric convention declared that a lance should be delivered in close combat couched under the arm.

the Greeks seem to have only partly married missile power with equine mobility.

In the 4th century BC, Xenophon, a cavalry commander, described the classic battle array of the Greek horse warrior.

'For harming the enemy we recommend the sabre [the famous Greek *kopis*] rather than the sword, because owing to his high position the rider will find the cut with the Persian sabre more effective than the thrust with the sword. In place of the spear with a long shaft, seeing that it is both weak and awkward to handle, we recommend two Persian javelins of cornel wood. The skilful man can throw one javelin and use the other in front or on either side or behind. We recommend throwing the javelin at the longest range possible. For this gives a man more time to turn his horse and to grasp the other javelin.'

The hurling of javelins became the characteristic battle tactic of all Western pre-Christian horse warriors, including those of the early Romans, the Celts, and the Germans. It is interesting to note also the considerable influence of Oriental Persian cavalry weaponry on the Greeks.

The nobility and high social stature of the horseman has been a characteristic of human society since prehistory. And nowhere more so than in cultures, like Europe, where horses were not as common as among the steppe peoples and so were especially symbolic of economic superiority. Among the Greeks, even though they raised the role of the foot soldier to new heights of battle efficiency and social acceptability, the superiority of

21

the horseman remained the same. Along the Parthenon Frieze all the 192 heroes of the battle of Marathon are portrayed on horseback, even though they would have fought as hoplites on foot, because in death they were to be accorded the greatest social status.

The same military hierarchy prevailed among the Celts. The Celts were the greatest European horsemen of the ancient world. Their talent for horsemanship allowed them to spread their culture from a heartland in central Europe to northern Italy, Spain, France, and Britain. The extent to which the Celts owed these conquests to their mounts was boldly demonstrated in southern Britain where they carved giant white horses in the chalk soil of hill sides, a sign of their superior horsemanship visible to natives for miles. Other cultures, especially the Romans, realised the value of Celtic horsemen and frequently employed them in their armies.

Although the Celts were influenced by the Greeks in economic and technical fields, their talent for riding ultimately derived from their ancient origin among the Aryan peoples of the steppes and this was maintained by their constant contact with the Cimmerians and then the Scythians in eastern Europe. Certainly, it was from the steppes that the Celts derived their famed passion for chariots. However, like the Greeks, the Celts never retained or adopted horse archery. Whatever the original reason for this, by the beginning of the first millennium AD it must have become

Norman horse warriors making a final assault on the Saxons at Hastings. In other battles, foot-soldiers in a strong defensive position fought off medieval cavalry. At Hastings, a superiority of tactics and morale counted more than Norman horsemanship. Painting by R. Caton Woodville.

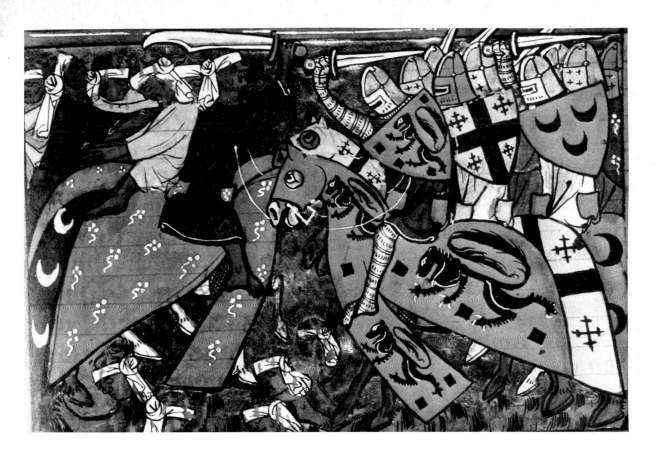

conventionalised as a social, aristocratic prejudice because the Germanic people, already greatly influenced by the military culture of the Celts, accepted also their view of the horse warrior as a carrier of sword and spear only. They did not subscribe to an orientalised Roman system in which all kinds of horsemen were employed as ordinary cavalry in a standing army. To the Celts and the Germans, horse warriors were not cavalry, but a social and martial élite, around whom an army was raised, not least because their poor economy ensured that only the nobility could afford sufficient horses and equipment.

In early medieval Europe, spear-throwing horse warriors continued to be the main means of combining missile power with horsemanship right up until the battle of Hastings. The Bayeux tapestry illustrates several Norman knights hurling their lances overarm at the Anglo-Saxons, while other comrades hold on to their lances for close combat. By this time, the knightly prejudice against horse archery was beginning to apply to those warriors who continued the primitive custom of throwing their lances. In Chretien de Troyes' 12th century saga of Perceval, the young hero is overwhelmed by his first sight of knights in dazzling, full armour. Of humble birth, Perceval believes they are angels and throws himself on the ground before them. The knights reassure the boy there is no need to fear them and the young hero immediately questions them about their arms.

23

'This is called a lance,' explains a knight.
'Do you throw it,' asks Perceval, 'as I do my javelins?'
'Certainly not! What a simpleton you are! You strike with it directly.'
'Then one of these three javelins I have is of greater worth, for with these I can kill as many birds or beasts as I wish with the full range of a crossbow.'
'Boy, that isn't my concern...'

The knight becomes irritated with such talk. As a noble warrior, he perceives the use of the thrown spear as acceptable only for simple huntsmen like the young Perceval.

Another reason has been suggested for the change in battle tactics from the lance thrown to the lance couched beneath the arm as a thrusting weapon. The introduction of the stirrup to Western Europe by the 9th century has often been seen as a major turning-point in cavalry history. But the stirrup was not rapidly adopted by all horse warriors and it did not dramtically change horse warfare. In the early days, many conservative horsemen considered it a sign of weakness. The transformation from throwing to holding a lance took centuries and was probably encouraged more by knightly prejudice than the introduction of the stirrup. Throughout the rest of the middle ages, the need for lance-throwing horsemen was transferred to the various kinds of light cavalry employed by medieval warlords.

Scenes from Scythian life. The upper drawing illustrates their horsemanship, the breaking and saddling of wild horses. From friezes on electrum vases of the 3rd or 4th centuries found north of the Black Sea, now in the Hermitage, Leningrad.

Photograph of a Mongolian horse archer of the late 19th century. His quiver carries a composite bow almost as long as himself.

The necessity of countering lightly armoured, skirmishing warriors encouraged the development of similar forces in support of the *coup de grâce* delivered by knights and their men-at-arms. The easiest method was to recruit direct from the opposition, but in addition to mercenaries, indigenous contingents of light horsemen were organised. In Britain, *hobelars* were raised to deal with the guerrilla attacks of the Welsh and Irish. 'Lightly armed men,' wrote Giraldus Cambrensis in the 12th century, 'should be used against an enemy who is lightly armed and mobile and who chooses to fight over rough terrain.' He drew a distinction between cavalry warfare in France on open plains and that in the densely wooded, mountainous land of Ireland and Wales. He advocated lightly armoured horsemen who could easily dismount to fight and were not confined in 'high and curved saddles'.

In Spain, the *reconquista* against the Muslims saw the development of

25

light horsemen deriving their name from their thoroughbred horses, *jinetes*. They rode low saddles with short stirrups and practised the feigned flight tactics of their Oriental opponents. In Italy in the 15th century, an influx of Albanian warriors ejected from the Turkish Balkans stimulated the development of *stradiots*. These fought as raiders with 12 foot lances tipped with iron at both ends as well as scimitars and heavy wooden clubs strapped to their saddles. When the French invaded Italy, they were terrified by these mail-clad Turkish-looking warriors, but soon learned to appreciate their value, and *stradiots* were regularly employed by French kings. Useful as these warriors were, none of them were horse archers.

It is time now to look at that other great horse culture we have referred to: the Oriental alternative to the Western cavalry tradition. Its home is the steppes of Eurasia. A land of long grass, and few trees, stretching from Hungary to China, populated only by nomads and their herds following a regular cycle of grazing, this was the birthplace of horse archery. The earliest Eurasian horsemen of whom we have a clear view are the Scythians. Their name derives from the Greeks who used it indiscriminately for all nomads of the Eurasian plains. It is from the Greeks that we also have our only written accounts of the Scythian way of life. Herodotus,

Irish chieftain attacking English knights, late 14th century. Like their Celtic ancestors, the Irish were noted for their light cavalry, which led to a belief in their military primitivism, hence the chieftain riding without stirrups.

26

Battle between German and Italian knights. On the left a knight wields a sword attached to his armour by a chain. From *Codex Balduineus*, 14th century.

who lived for a short while among the Scythians of the Black Sea, recounts the extent to which their attachment to their horses followed them into death. He describes the burial of a king.

'They strangle 50 of the dead king's servants and 50 of his best horses. They empty and cleanse the bellies of all and fill them with chaff. They then drive thick stakes lengthways through the horses' bodies to their necks and support the horses' shoulders and hindquarters on wheels attached to posts. Bridles and bits are placed in the horses' mouths and secured. Then they take each of the strangled young men and mount him on a horse with a stake. Having set horsemen like this all round the tomb, they ride away.'

Nearly 2,000 years later, the Mongols set up similar ghostly guardians around their royal burials.

The brilliance of Scythian horsemanship is revealed in a few relics uncovered in southern Russia. On the sides of an electrum jug of the 4th century BC, Scythian men endeavour to rope and control wild horses. Some of the horses have had their long manes clipped as a sign that they have been broken, while one Scythian seems about to untie the rope

27

hobbling a horse that is now fully harnessed and saddled. Remarkably, because of frozen tombs in central Asia, highly ornate Scythian harnesses have survived. At Pazirik, decorated leather saddles, saddle-cloths of felt, reins, bridles and bits have all been discovered. Most breath-taking of all are the antler-crowned headdresses intended to be worn by horses and elaborated with felt and copper and gilt hair. Another horse headdress is surmounted by the leather effigy of an ibex which in turn has a leather bird with gilt wings perched on its neck.

From the plains of central Asia, the influence of the Scythians and related tribes permeated the Eastern ancient world. Persian, Indian, and Chinese armies all recruited contingents of horse archers, many direct from the nomads. The military power of such horsemen was undeniable. Rome was reminded of their strength in the 4th century AD, when a new confederation of Eurasian tribes invaded the Eastern Empire. These were the Huns. Ammianus Marcellinus, a Roman officer, recorded the battle presence of these steppe warriors.

Indian horse and groom. The Mughals inherited the military horsemanship of their Turkish forefathers. Manuscript from north-west India, around 1660.

Russian horse warrior of the 16th century armed with bow, sabre and mace. The Russians remained a cavalry-orientated force so long as their chief enemies were the Tatars. From a painting by Schwartz, 1864.

'They are lightly equipped for swiftness. Unexpected in action, they divide suddenly into scattered bands and attack, rushing about chaotically, dealing terrible slaughter. Because of their extraordinary rapidity of movement, they are never seen to attack a rampart or pillage an enemy's camp. You would not hesitate to call them the most terrible of all warriors. They fight from a distance with arrows tipped with sharp bone. Then they gallop over the intervening spaces and fight hand to hand with swords, regardless of their own lives. And while the enemy are guarding against wounds from sabre cuts, they throw strips of cloth woven into nooses over their opponent and so entangle their limbs they cannot ride or walk.'

According to Ammianus, the Huns spent so much time on horseback they had difficulty walking. In battle, if ever dismounted, they considered themselves dead. Virtually every activity was conducted from horseback. Negotiations with Roman diplomats were nearly always debated in the saddle.

Around the 7th century, stirrups were in use among the Avars, a successor confederation to the Huns. A device originating in the Far East, it

29

Genghis Khan and his warriors clad in Persian armour. The horse archer in the bottom left shoots his bow backwards in typical steppe style. Persian miniature of the 16th century.

undoubtedly added to the stability of the horse-borne warrior, but it did not radically alter horsemanship on the steppes. Horse archers continued to dominate the wars and armies of Asia. Always a problem to the settled civilizations on its fringes, the Eurasian horse tribes seem to have reached a peak of organisation and military efficiency within the hordes of the Mongols. In the 13th century, the Mongols invaded Poland and tested Western horsemanship at the battle of Liegnitz.

The northern European princes assembled an army comprised largely of

Heavily armoured Persian and Turanian armies confront each other. Middle Eastern armies consisted almost entirely of cavalry. Persian miniature of the 15th century.

hastily recruited, unprofessional feudal levies. At its core, however, was a splendid array of northern knighthood including the warriors of the Teutonic Order. With this force behind him, Duke Henry of Silesia advanced upon the raiding Mongols. Marco Polo describes the classic steppe tactics that confronted them.

'When the Tatars engage in battle they never mix with the enemy, but keep hovering about him, discharging their arrows first from one side and then from the

other. Occasionally they pretend to retreat, but during their flight, shoot backwards at their pursuers, killing men and horses as though they were fighting face to face. In this sort of warfare the adversary imagines he has gained a victory, when in fact he has lost the battle. The Tatars observe the damage they have done him, wheel about, and renew the fight, overwhelming his remaining troops.'

When Duke Henry saw the Mongols retreat at the battle of Liegnitz, he did indeed believe he was in sight of victory. The Teutonic knights and all his other heavy horsemen thundered forward. The lightly clad Mongol horse archers scattered before them and reformed on their flanks. Suddenly, hails of arrows plunged into the sides and front of the charging knights as the Mongol centre further enticed them in among their warriors. Smoke bombs were then hurled through the air to land behind the Western knights, thus screening them from the rest of their amazed army. In the chaos and smoke, the Oriental horse archers maintained their murderous rain while more heavily armed horsemen rode in for the kill. At the end of the day, most of the Teutonic knights lay dead as well as many other top chivalric figures. The Mongols recorded the number of enemy dead by cutting an ear from every body: nine large sacks of these gruesome trophies were delivered to their leader.

Tilting at the quintain, knights practise their martial horsemanship. Facsimile of a miniature from the *Chroniques de Charlemagne*, 14th century.

Gothic horse-armour and knight. Made at Landshut around 1485, it demonstrates the continuing powerful presence of the armoured horse warrior in the late Middle Ages. Now in the Wallace Collection, London.

With the fragmentation of the Mongol Empire in the late Middle Ages, no steppe confederation ever posed such an overwhelming threat to its neighbours. Nevertheless, the horsemen of the plains remained fiercely independent and their raids proved a relentless problem:

'I fear the Tatars most of all,' said the Ottoman Sultan Selim I in the 16th century. 'They are as fast as the wind upon their enemies. When they march they cover five or six days' road in one day, and when they retreat they disappear as quickly. Especially important is the fact that their horses do not require shoes, nails or fodder. When they come to a river they do not wait for a boat like our troops. Their food, like their bodies, is nothing much. Their strength is shown by the fact that they do not care for comfort.'

In the 17th century, Crimean Tatars regularly rode against the Poles and Russians in major pillaging campaigns. They were met by footsoldiers armed with firearms and initially Tatar armies were broken by a volley of gunfire. But they soon learned the ineffectiveness of such muskets and their horsemen charged into the field of fire 'as though it had robbed them of their sight'. Well into the 18th century, the Tatars' composite bow had a longer range than most firearms. It was against these warriors that the Russian Cossacks perfected their particular style of fighting. By the 19th

Louis XII leaving Alexandria to punish the city of Genoa, 1507. The brilliant appearance of knights on the field of battle had an impact as important as their military prowess. From a miniature by Jean Marot, now in the Bibliothèque Nationale, Paris.

century, however, the role of the horse archers was no longer secure and their contribution to military culture declined. The majority of Eastern armies adopted the cavalry tactics and organisation of the West. That said, some of the old ways of the Tatars remained to confront Western Imperialists. In 1860, during the Second Opium War, British and French soldiers introduced Chinese Tatars to the devastating effect of new technology.

'The mandarin in command was seen riding up and down in front of his men,' recalls a 19th century British account, 'urging them to the charge; and when we came within two hundred yards of them, the Tatars gave a series of shrill yells, and spurring up the bank charged furiously, firing and slinging their matchlocks as they came on. The general and staff instantly galloped to the flanks, uncovering the Armstrongs, which were wheeled round in hot haste, the limbers cast-off and the muzzles levelled. The Tatars had an idea that the Allies were panicstricken, thus they came on the more boldly, whooping and yelling their war-cries; but before they had proceeded far, the case-shot swept through them, and their cheers gave place to cries of rage and despair; and a volley from the rifles of the 2nd Queen's forced them to retire.'

Firearms had already presented a new challenge to Western horse warriors by the 15th century, especially European knighthood. As with the bow, they admitted its usefulness, but declined to use it themselves. The dishonour of employing a missile weapon was compounded by the fact that those professional soldiers expert in the use of guns were frequently despised foreign mercenaries. Or, as Anthoine de la Salle said of a dead knight at Naples in 1438, he was killed by gunners who were 'only artisans by trade'. The destruction of valiant warlords was decried, but there was little attempt to ban firearms and towards the end of the century large numbers of gunners on foot and mounted were recruited alongside bowmen. Indeed, far from shutting their eyes to firearms, many medieval nobles took a lively interest in their artillery trains and incorporated guns into their coats of arms. But that is not to say they regarded the gun as a chivalric means of dispatching the foe and even into the 16th century, few knights careful of their honour would handle a gun on the field of battle. Lance and sword remained the principal arms of the fully armoured horse warrior of the 16th century.

The 15th century has often been viewed as the waning of the European Middle Ages, with the persistence of the knight warrior into the 16th century a positive anachronism, maintained not for military efficiency but for social reasons. As has been emphasised in this chapter, social status did influence greatly the manner of fighting among European knights, but their presence in 15th and 16th century armies was for sound military reasons. Indeed, it was not a case of survival, but a blossoming. For by this time, the crisis of Western medieval warfare had been resolved. The pikemen and bowmen that had inflicted shock defeats on the knights of the 14th century had now been incorporated successfully into the armies of leading warlords. Along with artillery, firearms, and light cavalry, they were considered a vital arm of any late medieval army. But equally important were the heavily armoured horsemen consisting of knights and their similarly attired men-at-arms. They were the core of every army, not least because their social position provided its officers and their money the majority of its arms, but also because at the climax of a battle they could provide the winning blow, both in the power of their arms and the psychological impact of their presence.

Knights had long ago learned they could not determine a battle alone, but as one arm of a flexible battle array they were essential. That is why, in 1494, over half of the French army that invaded Italy was composed of heavily armoured horsemen. 'It was the Gendarmerie which was always the strength of the army,' wrote Gabriel Daniel in his 18th century history of French cavalry, 'as much by the goodness of its arms as by the strength

German horsemen armed with pistols and carbines. They replaced mounted crossbowmen as the most effective medium armoured cavalry of the Renaissance. From Jost Amman's *Kunstbüchlin*, 1599.

of its warhorses.' And largely that was true. The majority of knights had been trained from an early age in warfare. Their pursuit of honour as a social virtue meant they were committed to outperforming their comrades in battle. Their wealth insisted they spend lavishly on the finest weapons, armour, and horses. Their fascination with finely wrought suits of armour was not late medieval decadence, but a realisation that strength and protection must be combined with an impressive appearance to fully capitalise on their impact on the battlefield. It is interesting to note that the total weight of equipment carried by a knight around 1480 (that is, armour and saddlery, approximately 150 lb, 68 kg) was half that carried by a German cuirassier of 1909 (whose equipment weighed 334 lb, 151·5 kg), or a British Household Cavalryman in 1875 (308 lb, 139·7 kg). Indeed, Maurice de Saxe in the 18th century could not understand why the heavy cavalry of his day did not retain full armour. It was an excellent defence against sword cuts and all but direct shot. He believed it was expense and discomfort that had discouraged its use, not the presence of firearms. Besides, French cavalry had worn armour up until the 1660s. He proposed a reintroduction of armoured regiments. Impervious to sword cuts, they would receive the first volley of enemy gunfire against their armour and once this had proved as ineffective as it usually was, they would then charge home in the manner of the old Gendarmerie. Saxe was no fantasist. He won a series of major victories in the 1740s and was Marshal of France.

Through realising their still potent role within armies of the 15th and 16th centuries, knights and men-at-arms had ceased to be a gang of individuals at odds with their social inferiors, but had developed a specialised role for themselves that would continue in later centuries under the title of heavy cavalry. The character, however, of this essentially aristocratic force was to remain as hidebound and snobbish as it had been in the Middle Ages. Pistols were accepted by heavy cavalry in the 17th century as a necessary arm, but there was still a considerable gap in prestige between an armoured horseman armed with pistol and sword, whose role culminated in the charge and close combat, and the light cavalryman as scout and raider, or the dragoon who carried a musket and might be expected to fight on foot. The old prejudices remained strong. The sense of honour that prevented Germanic horsemen from using bows at the siege of Rome in the 6th century had long ago established the hierarchy of horse warriors that would continue to dominate the development of Western European cavalry from the 17th century onwards. It even contributed, somewhere deep down inside, to the revulsion of senior army men in the early 20th century to the introduction of the tank.

2 · DRAGOON, HUSSARS AND LANCERS

Western European cavalry developed its regimental formations and traditional duties and differences in the 17th and 18th centuries. Powerful military leaders and outstanding captains of cavalry such as Gustavus Adolphus, Cromwell, Marlborough, Frederick the Great and von Seydlitz drilled and dressed their dragoons, cuirassiers and hussars into brilliant and victorious condition. These leaders inspired loyalty, bravery – and change. The period of the English Civil War saw the introduction of significant military changes. It was then that English horse soldiers began to distinguish themselves as the decisive factor on the battle field.

The cavalry encounters between Cromwell and Prince Rupert provided a number of lessons for leaders of horse. Oliver Cromwell, in his 40s when he first drew a sword, proved himself a remarkable soldier from the start of his late military career. He himself raised, organised and disciplined his troops of horse and set his men an example they were quick to follow. Cromwell's 'mental and bodily energy,' wrote Captain Nolan of Light Brigade fame, 'his vigorous conceptions, quick decisions and the dread vehemence with which he urged his war-steed into the thick of battle made him a cavalry leader second to none in history'.

Prince Rupert of the Rhine, Cromwell's fiery adversary, sported plenty of cavalier dash and courage, mixed with equal quantity of rashness and impetuosity. Thus he was no match for the cool, calculating Cromwell (twenty years Rupert's senior) who often turned impending defeat into victory, whereas the reckless prince ruined many triumphant opportunities by allowing his careering cavalry to get out of order after an initial success. Edgehill – the first major battle of the war, 23 October 1642 – is a good example of Rupert's shortfall as a cavalry leader. His horsemen charged and routed the Parliamentary cavalry and pursued them off the field.

'Just before we began our march [charge]', recorded a Royalist horseman, 'Prince Rupert passed from one wing to the other, giving positive orders to the horse to march as close as was possible, keeping their ranks with sword in hand, to receive the enemy's shot without firing either carbine or pistol till we broke in amongst the enemy, and then to make use of our firearms as need should require, which order was punctually observed.'

Rupert's tactics were inspired by his experience in the army which had been created by Gustavus Adolphus, the Swedish King who brought

Prince Rupert of the Rhine. A dashing, often successful leader of Royalist cavalry, but his reckless, impulsive nature ruined a number of triumphant opportunities.

40

Oliver Cromwell, wearing, for the purpose of this martial portrait, three-quarter armour, which at the time of the English Civil War was going out of fashion.

change in the use of cavalry by fully exploiting the power of horse mobility and shock contact in close combat. The advent of pistol and carbine led Gustavus to devise a combined system of firepower and sabre attack. He attached musketeers on foot to his cavalry units; these soldiers, with longer range than the mounted pistoleers, blasted a gap in the enemy ranks through which the Swedish cavalry could dash and use pistols and blades effectively at close quarters.

It seems that a 17th century cavalry charge was delivered at a sharp trot rather than at the gallop (as indeed it appears to have obtained throughout the succeeding history of heavy cavalry), therefore the 'march' referred to at Edgehill can be interpreted as the charge. Having routed the inferior Roundhead cavalry, Rupert's cavaliers pursued the fleeing horsemen off the field for some two miles and, on reaching the town of Kineton, set about pillaging the Parliamentary baggage train. Rupert managed to rally a few troops of his disorganised horsemen and return to the battle field, where the Earl of Essex launched his Roundheads in a fierce counterattack and the battle ended indecisively. Had Rupert contained his cavalry from

41

The battle of Ivry, 1590, in which Henry of Navarre, sporting the white helmet plume, leads a charge against the forces of the Catholic League. These heavy horsemen wear three-quarter cuirassier armour.

Cromwell at Marston Moor, a battle in which his cavalry acumen won the day. Illustration by R. Caton Woodville.

headlong pursuit and deployed them to advantage on the field the King would surely have enjoyed a complete victory. Cromwell and his troop arrived too late at Edgehill to be particularly engaged. He made the following observation to John Hampden as they left the field:

'Your troops are mostly old dependent servants, wine boosers and similar scum, those of the enemy the sons of gentlemen, young men of rank. Can you believe that the spirit of such rabble can compare with that of men who fight for honour, with determination in their hearts? You must raise men of spirit that are likely to go on as far as gentlemen will go, or else they will be beaten still.'

Cromwell's own troop consisted of hand-picked men, God-fearing, abstemious, and ready to die for their beliefs; the disciplined nucleus of the celebrated 'Ironsides'. The cavaliers who formed the Royalist horse were

43

little different in status and manner from the noble horse warriors of
previous centuries. They were mostly gentlemen of rank accompanied by
servants, expert in riding and hunting and eager to seize upon the chase or
pursuit. What they lacked in military discipline they made up in
horsemanship, courage inspired by loyalty and honour, and wealth of
arms. Other king's horsemen, of lower social status, were termed dragoons
and dismounted to fire their muskets or carbines.

Cromwell, born in 1599 of yeoman stock and educated at Cambridge,
received his first commission in September 1642 as captain of a Troop of
Horse, the strength of a troop being then fixed at one captain, one
lieutenant, one cornet (who carried the cornet or flag), one quartermaster,
and 60 horses. In February 1643 he was promoted to colonel with
command of 14 troops, whom he kept constantly at drill. Cromwell
believed fervently in discipline, both spiritual and martial, and trained his
Ironsides hard, seeing also that they were promptly paid, well provisioned
and equipped – 'If a man has not good weapons, horse, and harness, he is
as nought' said Cromwell. His methods forged a model regiment and his
kind of training and organisation was influential in the forming of
Parliament's New Model Army of 1645.

Cromwell first encountered Royalist cavalry at Grantham in May 1643.
He commanded 12 troops against the enemy's 21 troops of horse and 4 of
dragoons. They formed at musket-shot range from each other, the

Battle of Marston Moor, 2 July 1644.
Illustration by John de Walton.

45

dragoons firing for 30 minutes or more. Then Cromwell led his troopers in a charge (or as he described it, 'a pretty round trot') which the enemy received standing. 'By God's providence they were immediately routed,' Cromwell reported, 'and we had the execution of them for two or three miles.' At Marston Moor, near York, on 2 July 1644 Cromwell, now lieutenant general, commanded the cavalry on the left wing of the Scots-Parliamentary army and found himself opposed by Prince Rupert with a similar number of horsemen.

Both sides formed their lines of battle in the conventional order of the day – cavalry on the wings and infantry in the centre. The opposing forces were drawn up on sloping ground with a ditch between. At first neither side would give up the advantage which the ditch gave to those on the defensive until Cromwell broke the deadlock and attacked.

'We came down the hill', wrote Watson, Cromwell's master of scouts, 'in the bravest order and greatest resolution that ever was seen. In a moment we were

Typical cavalry dress of the English Civil War. Short cuirass (body armour) over stout leather jacket and helmet with triple-bar face guard and laminated tail protecting the neck. Note the single metal gauntlet on the left arm.

LIGHT HORSEMAN.
Temp. Oliver Cromwell.
Figure in collection of Captain Orde Browne.

Cromwell's Ironsides versus Rupert's Cavaliers, from a painting by Harry Payne.

passed the ditch on to the moor upon equal terms with the enemy. Our front division charged their front, Cromwell's own division of 300 horses, in which *he himself was in person*, charging the first division of Prince Rupert's of which *himself was in person* in which all were gallant men. A flank attack by other of Rupert's squadrons for the moment brought Cromwell to a standstill, and though they returned to the attack they were again repulsed by Rupert's own Lifeguards; but the Ironsides pressed hard and Rupert's soldiers were forced apart.'

Cromwell had kept part of his cavalry in reserve and these, at a critical moment, joined the battle and put Rupert's men to flight. 'The Prince of Plunderers, invincible heretofore,' says a jubilant Watson, 'first tasted the steel of Oliver's Ironsides and did not in the least like it.' The Royalist right wing, pursued by horse and foot, was driven far back. However, the exact counterpart to this had taken place on the opposite wings of the contending armies. The Royalist left wing had attacked and driven back the right wing of Parliament's army, defeating the horsemen, who in galloping to the rear spread confusion and dismay amongst the reserves of Scots infantry. When Cromwell learned of this he at once collected his cavalry from the pursuit, wheeled about and followed the victorious Royalists, who formed up to receive him and were defeated and fled. Thus 'stout Cromwell redeemed the day'.

His cavalry tactics also secured victory at Naseby on 14th June 1645 where Rupert commanded the Royalist right wing, Sir Marmaduke Langdale the left, Lord Astley the main body, with King Charles I in person heading the reserve. Cromwell commanded the right wing of Parliament's

In the battle of Naseby, 14 June 1645, Henry Ireton, commanding Parliament's left wing, charged deep into the enemy. His horse was shot dead under him and he suffered several wounds and was momentarily taken prisoner.

army, Ireton the left, Fairfax and Skippon the main body. Rupert charged the left wing, drove the Roundheads through the streets of Naseby village and continued the pursuit, the headlong chase beloved by the cavaliers. Cromwell, at the same time, marched against the Royal horse under Langdale and put them to flight. The Royal infantry, in the meantime, were driving back the Parliamentary foot soldiers.

The fate of the day depended upon which side should first see their cavalry return from the pursuit. Cromwell at once reformed his Ironsides, leaving a small force with fresh horses to continue the chase, and charged the flank of the advancing King's infantry, trampling them into confusion and retreat. Charles fled the field, leaving his artillery and 5,000 of his men captive. When Rupert, his horses blown and his men in disorder, returned to the battlefield, Cromwell fell upon them with closed squadrons of fresh horses and in two successive charges dispersed and destroyed the cavaliers, pursuing them 14 miles to the gates of Leicester. There are few occasions in history in which cavalry has been employed to better purpose than by Cromwell at Naseby.

After Charles I was executed in 1649 his son Prince Charles, later Charles II, continued the war and following his defeat in the field by Cromwell, fled to the Continent in 1651. A number of Royalists accompanied him into exile and, in Holland, 80 of them were formed into a royal mounted bodyguard. On the restoration of the British monarchy in 1660 Charles II's mounted bodyguard was increased to 600, organised into three troops of Horse Guards. In 1788 the Horse Guards were disbanded and reformed as the 1st and 2nd Regiments of Life Guards; in 1928 the units amalgamated to become the single regiment of The Life Guards and remains so today, the senior regiment of the British Army. The Life Guards and The Blues and Royals today form the Household Cavalry, troops dressed in the full panoply of Victorian cavalry who provide the Sovereign's Escort on state and ceremonial occasions. They are not, however, toy soldiers, but a fully integrated part of the British Army, equipped with armoured cars and tanks, ready to serve anywhere they are required.

The Royal Horse Guards (The Blues) were directly descended from the Regiment of Horse which Cromwell ordered to be raised in Newcastle and County Durham in 1650. After the restoration Charles retained the regiment but replaced its Parliamentary officers with his own, and the regiment was named the Royal Regiment of Horse Guards; the nickname 'The Blues' referred to their blue coats; the Life Guards wear red. In 1969 The Blues amalgamated with the Royal Dragoons (1st Dragoons), the resulting regiment being named The Blues and Royals.

In central Europe, the testing ground of military efficiency remained the borderland with the Turks. In 1683, the Ottoman army had advanced through Hungary into Austria and now laid siege to Vienna. The Holy Roman Emperor Leopold fled to Passau, now in Bavaria, with barely 10,000 florins left in his coffers. Christendom was on the verge of catastrophe. The Pope stepped in with financial support but still troops had

The Royalists lost the day at Naseby. King Charles, shown here, wanted to personally lead his horse guards in a counterattack but was prevented from riding to his death by the Earl of Carnwath.

Officer of the Tangier Horse regiment raised in 1661 to defend the new British possession of Tangier. This regiment became the 1st (Royal) Dragoons in 1751. Painting by Richard Simkin.

to be raised. As the Islamic hordes assembled outside their city, the citizens of Vienna despaired. They fired rockets into the night sky for help. Little did they know that far away in Poland, John Sobieski was mobilising forces to stem the Turkish tide. By the 12th September, the King of Poland and his allies were in the suburbs of Vienna. The armies that clashed that day outside the city walls included the most brilliant and terrifying horsemen of Eastern Europe.

The Polish army of the late 17th century was essentially a cavalry army. In countless wars against Russians, Cossacks, and Tartars, the Poles had

been compelled to meet these swift-moving raiders from the steppes with similarly equipped horse warriors. At the heart of the Polish cavalry were the *husaria* or hussars. These were not light horsemen, like Hungarian hussars, but were heavy cavalry – among the most splendidly attired in Europe. Coming from the noblest ranks, they wore three-quarter plate armour over which was slung a leopard-skin cloak. As if this were not enough, to the plate armour which they wore on their backs was attached gilded wooden wings filled with eagle feathers. In battle, it was said the wind rushed through the wings of the horsemen making a terrifying wailing sound. The armoury carried by each hussar included a sabre, a straight sword, a battle-hammer, two pistols, and a 15 foot lance. In support of the *husaria* rode Polish Cossacks. They wore bascinet helmets and mail shirts, and wielded sabres, lances, pistols and composite bows. An intermediate, more heavily armoured category were the *pancerny*. Finally, there were always contingents of totally unarmoured light cavalry in order to scout and harass the enemy. Used to battles against Eastern horsemen, the Polish army frequently employed similar shock tactics against Western

enemies. At the beginning of the 17th century, Polish cavalry charged upon Swedish armies with their sabres flashing in a manner that is said to have been the inspiration for Gustavus Adolphus' cavalry reforms.

The Turkish cavalry that confronted the Poles and Austro-Germans outside Vienna were no less impressive. The regular horsemen were called *sipahi* and these included mailclad heavy cavalry, light cavalry, and foreign horsemen from throughout their Empire. Ogier Ghiselin de Busbecq, German Ambassador at Constantinople, described his impressions of a Turkish cavalryman a century earlier.

'The Turkish horseman presents a very elegant spectacle, mounted on a horse of Cappadocian or Syrian or some other good breed, with trappings and horse-cloths of silver spangled with gold and precious stones. He is resplendent in raiment of cloth of gold and silver, or else of silk or satin, or at any rate of the finest scarlet, or violet, or dark green cloth. At either side is a fine sheath, one to hold the bow, the other full of bright-coloured arrows, both of wonderful Babylonian workmanship, as also is the ornamented shield which is attached to the left arm and which is only suited to ward off arrows and the blows dealt by a club or sword. His right hand is encumbered by a light spear, usually painted green, unless he prefers to keep that hand free; and he is girt with a scimitar studded with gems, while a steel club hangs from his horse-cloth or saddle.'

To these arms, in the late 17th century, can be added a pair of pistols or a carbine.

52

The opening phase of the relief of Vienna was a gruelling manoeuvring through forest and suburban buildings, and across entrenchments. Against the Janissaries and *sipahi*, John Sobieski and his Austro-German allies combined infantry, artillery, and cavalry. Each arm aided the other and strengthened their resolve. By late afternoon, Sobieski and the generals wondered whether they should pause and save the final blow for the next

Turkish cavalryman with crescent and star pennant.

Types of Russian, Hungarian and Polish soldiers of the 16th century.

day. But the aggression of their soldiers and the wavering of the Turks convinced them this was a crucial stage. It was time now for an attack of such overwhelming power it would devastate the Turks once and for all. Sobieski sent orders to his cavalry to remount and advance all together. The *husaria* raised their eagle wings and 15 foot lances. The *pancerny* unsheathed their sabres and cocked their carbines. They assembled in a chess board formation: the *husaria* in front for impact, the *pancerny* behind them in the intervals for fire-power. The horsemen trotted forward, slowly gathering speed.

Sobieski rode in the lead, astride a handsome dun, his helmet decorated with a brilliant feather secured by a jewel clasp. He held the *bulawa*, a gilded baton of command containing a dagger. Beside him rode his son: unarmoured, he wielded a sabre and carried a dagger thrust beneath his

54

The Duke of Marlborough and
Prince Eugene of Savoy, allies in the
War of the Spanish Succession,
shown here reconnoitring. From an
engraving by Camsvelt.

saddle in the Polish manner. Next to him was a hussar brandishing the *bunczuk*, a massive heraldic lance decorated with bright feathers and ribbons. Behind them cantered princely aristocrats adorned in the finest armour. It was the most remarkable array of horsemen in Europe at that time. The entire cavalry force, said to number 20,000, urged their horses onward. A stretch of rough ground and vineyards slowed the advance, but once they burst into the clear, the Turks were confronted and the charge smashed home. Lances were heard to shatter. The Turks were bundled back into their camp. Sobieski and his *husaria* captured the artillery. The Turkish left flank disintegrated, soon to be joined by the rest of their army, scrabbling for a way out across the Vienna River. The more reckless cavalry were tempted to follow, but it was getting dark and Sobieski was wary of a counter-attack. Besides, Vienna was liberated and a major victory had already been secured for Christian Europe. Never again would the Turks venture so far. Above all, the Polish cavalry had proved they were among the finest in Europe. They established a reputation for Polish lancers which

fascinated the West for over a century. However, despite their success, Western European armies waited until Napoleon acknowledged their use on Western battlefields before they included lancers in their own cavalry.

Towards the end of the 17th century, the invention of the bayonet made the pike extinct, while the flintlock musket increased the firepower of the ordinary infantryman. Both developments were initiated by the French, the superpower of Europe. But in spite of such innovation, their approach to the use of cavalry seemed far behind. They still believed in the effect of a pistol volley delivered from horseback. Certainly, a series of victories in major battles did little to contradict this. In Britain, however, the spirit of Cromwell remained dominant. Both practices were to be tested at the opening of the 18th century in the War of the Spanish Succession. When the Duke of Marlborough led his *mélange* of allied warriors to southern

The battle of Hochstadt and Blenheim, 13 August 1704. In the right foreground Prince Eugene points his sword to direct the attack on Ober-Glauheim in the centre of the picture. On the left in the distance can be seen Blenheim in flames, and Marlborough attacking with his cavalry.

Germany against the ambitions of Louis XIV, he gave his cavalry strict instructions. 'He would not allow the horse but three charges of powder and ball to each man for a campaign,' recorded General Kane, 'and that only for guarding their horses when at grass and not to be made use of in action.' To protect his men against French firearms, he reintroduced the breastplate.

Marlborough demonstrated his system to good effect at Blenheim over the French and Bavarians in 1704. In a day in which all elements of his army were splendidly co-ordinated, he held in reserve 6,000 cavalry for a final, decisive charge. In a double line of squadrons three miles long, Marlborough's allied horsemen trotted forward and increased speed as they approached the lines of the *Maison du Roi* (the French Household Cavalry). The French raised their pistols and fired, emptying many saddles, but the remainder dashed on through the smoke and ran into the French. Under the flailing allied blades the *Maison du Roi* and their comrades broke and fled.

When Frederick the Great became King of Prussia in 1740 he inherited a large army of tall parade-ground soldiers, the marching pride of his

eccentric father King Frederick William. The new King viewed these martial giants, especially the cavalry, with a critical eye: 'The heavy cavalry consisted, like the infantry, of very big men mounted on monstrous horses. These colossi on elephants, however, could neither manoeuvre nor fight. No parade went by without some of them falling off. The officers had no conception of cavalry service.' Frederick transformed the Prussian cavalry into the finest in Europe, and, commanded by brilliant leaders like Friedrich Wilhelm von Seydlitz and Hans Joachim von Zieten, Frederick's squadrons dealt decisive blows in battles such as Rossbach, Leuthen, and Freiberg.

The new King believed in practical training and drill in cavalry shock. He instructed his cavalry that once committed to the charge they should not use firearms but must rely on the sword. Above all Frederick believed in attack, the Prussians must always be first to attack, after which cavalry

Prussian dragoons of 1740. From a painting by R. Knotel.

commanders must reform their squadrons as quickly as possible for further cohesive action. In 1748 Frederick required his cavalry to charge over 700 yards: 300 at the trot and 400 at the gallop. In 1750 the demand rose to 1,200 yards: 300 at the trot, 400 gallop, remainder full speed. In 1755 this was upped to 1,800 yards, with the last 600 at full speed. Frederick usually rode in these training attacks himself, to satisfy himself of the speed and execution, and thought nothing of repeating the exercise twice, three or more times if necessary to reach the required standard.

'I make the squadrons charge at a fast gallop,' Frederick once explained, 'because then fear carries the faint-hearted along with the rest; they know that if they hesitate in the middle of the onrush they will be crushed by the rest of the squadron.'

Three types of cavalry dominated Frederick's army: the cuirassier, the dragoon, and the hussar. The cuirassiers formed the heavy cavalry, the shock element, and were used to strike the initial or decisive blow that hopefully would shatter the enemy lines. These big men on big horses wore an iron breastplate (the cuirass) and carried a heavy sword, a pair of pistols and a carbine. Cuirassiers in Frederick's time (and in other armies over the next century) were not expected to do outpost duty, foraging, nor reconnoitring. They represented the cavalry's mailed fist.

Dragoons were classed as medium cavalry, and this was reflected in the size of the man and his horse. Originally intended as mounted infantry, combining the mobility of cavalry with the firepower of foot soldiers, dragoons in Frederick's army (and in other forces over the years) besides fighting dismounted were often employed in regular cavalry actions. They did not wear body armour and were armed with pistols, carbine and sword.

The battle of Ramillies, 23 May 1706. Another victory for Marlborough. The cavalry action as depicted by the Victorian artist R. Caton Woodville.

The Duke of Marlborough leading the cavalry at the battle of Oudenarde in 1708 in which he defeated the French.

60

The term 'dragoon' is said to derive from *dragon*, a short musket (that 'breathed fire like a dragon') first carried by French horse soldiers in the 16th century.

The hussars formed the light cavalry; speedy horsemen required to carry out a variety of duties, they watched over the safety of the army, in advance, on the flanks, and in the rear, to prevent surprise attack. They reconnoitred, raided, and pursued the fleeing enemy. And when the situation demanded it, hussars charged with the heavy cavalry. These dashing light horsemen were modelled on the Hungarian *huszar* employed by the Austrian army, horsemen celebrated for their colourful and swaggering dress. Hussar regiments came to be raised in most Western European armies and in the British army.

Frederick the Great was well served by the remarkable young cavalry officer Friedrich Wilhelm von Seydlitz. He was 33 when he led the Prussian

'Life in Paris, 1793' painted by Francois Flameng, showing a handsome hussar wearing his fur-edged pelisse or outer-jacket slung over his shoulder.

Painting by Harry Payne depicting the 2nd Dragoons, Royal Scots Greys at various periods. Top left: a private of 1704. Top right: a private of 1742. Middle: a private of 1815. Bottom left: an officer of 1799. Bottom right: an officer and private of 1811.

Types of cavalrymen in Frederick the Great's army.
Left to right: hussar officer, a cuirassier and a private of the mounted grenadiers.

cavalry at the battle of Rossbach in 1757. Employing the aggressive cavalry initiative that so pleased Frederick, Seydlitz read the developing situation perfectly and moved on the Austro-French enemy without waiting for, or seeking, specific orders. Trotting, then cantering forward, Seydlitz suddenly threw his tobacco pipe into the air as the signal to charge. A French officer described the impact:

'Barely had we formed up, when the whole of the Prussian cavalry advanced compact like a wall and at an incredible speed. With its right it attacked the Austrian cavalry, which was in column and was unable to place in battle more than three of four squadrons. With its left it charged us.'

64

General Loudon's Austrian cavalry charge the Prussians at Kunersdorf in 1759 during the Seven Years' War. Frederick's army pursued the Austro-Russian forces too far; the enemy rallied and defeated the Prussians.

Friedrich Wilhelm von Seydlitz, brilliant Prussian cavalry leader who secured a number of victories for Frederick the Great.

Seydlitz had pounced while the enemy was still advancing in column – a classic flank attack. The enemy wavered and many fled. Frederick now supported the achievements of his horsemen with terrific firepower. 'The artillery tore down whole ranks of us. The Prussian musketry did terrible execution.' The enemy could not deploy and in the confusion the battle was won. Seydlitz regrouped and led the pursuit of the routed allied army; a manhunt in which the hussars were relentless. Seydlitz and the cavalry had saved the day at Rossbach, where Frederick's army of 21,000 men faced an Austro-French strength of 64,000. Some years later when

French cavalryman of 1766 armed with sabre, a brace of pistols and a carbine. Illustration from *The Uniforms of the King's Household Troops and all the French Regiments* by De Monsigny.

A saxon cuirassier of the Napoleonic Wars.

Frederick criticised the seat of the cavalry in a review, Seydlitz took the liberty of answering: 'Majesty, they are riding in the same style as they did at Rossbach.'

Both Napoleon and Wellington employed heavy cavalry *en masse* as the shock element at critical times in battle: to trample a broken infantry square, to exploit a gap, to turn a flank, to bully and intimidate the enemy. Napoleon's heavy cavalry consisted mainly of cuirassier and carabinier regiments; both types of horsemen wore metal helmet and breastplate, carried sabre and a brace of pistols, and rode a large horse. Advancing in dense formation, riding knee to knee, these big and ponderous cavalry-

Helmet of a Captain of French dragoons, late 18th century.

FIRST, or
KING's
Dragoon Guards,
COMMANDED BY
Gen. Sir Wm. Augustus Pitt, K.B.

A FEW
DASHING LADS
ARE NOW WANTED,

To complete the above well-known Regiment to a New Eſtabliſhment.

Any YOUNG MAN who is deſirous to make a Figure in Life, and wiſhes to quit a dull laborious Retirement in the Country, has now an Opportunity of entering at once into that glorious State of Eaſe and Independence, which he cannot fail to enjoy in the

KING's DRAGOON GUARDS.

The ſuperior Comforts and Advantages of a Dragoon in this Regiment, need only be made known to be generally coveted

All Young Men who have their own Intereſt at Heart, and are fortunate enough to make this diſtinguiſhed Regiment their Choice are requeſted to apply immediately to

Serj. TIBBLES, at the Angel Inn, Honiton,
WHERE THEY WILL RECEIVE

The Higheſt Bounty
And all the Advantages of a Dragoon.

As Recruits are now flocking in from all Quarters, no Time is to be loſt; and it is hoped that no young Man will ſo far neglect his own Intereſt as not embrace the glorious Opportunity without Delay

N. B. This Regiment is ſuppoſed to be mounted on the moſt beautiful, fine, active black Geldings this Country ever produced.

The Bringer of a good Recruit will receive a Reward of Three Guineas.

EXETER. PRINTED BY TRIWMAN AND SON, HIGHSTREET

Recruiting poster, circa 1800, setting forth the advantages of becoming a member of the King's Dragoon Guards.

men, breastplate and blades flashing, rarely moved into battle faster than a trot, 'The first time a body of cuirassiers approached the square,' a British officer wrote of Waterloo, 'the men [in the square] – all young soldiers – seemed to be alarmed. They fired high with little effect.' And Sergeant Morris recalled:

'A considerable number of French cuirassiers made their appearance on the rising ground just in our front, took the artillery we had placed there and came at a gallop [fast trot] down upon us. Their appearance was certainly enough to inspire a feeling of dread. None of them under six feet, defended by steel helmets and breastplates, made pigeon-breasted to throw off the musket balls. The appearance was of such a formidable nature that I thought we could not have the slightest chance with them.'

Wellington's heavy horsemen comprised the Household Cavalry (the Life Guards and Royal Horse Guards) and the regiments of Dragoon Guards. The bulk of Napoleon's medium cavalry consisted of dragoons, horsemen trained in infantry drill to be employed when necessary in the role of foot soldier. The French light horse – chiefly hussars and chasseurs – carried out the duties already mentioned. A number of British light dragoon regiments were converted to hussars and these, like the hussars of other nations, retained the distinctive braided dolman (jacket) and fur-edged pelisse (outer jacket) of the Hungarian paradigm. When not worn as a jacket the pelisse was slung over the shoulder in swashbuckling style.

A trooper of the 16th (Queen's) Lancers in marching order, late 1890s. Note the modified *chapska* lance-cap.

German lancers of Saxony, 1814-20 period, from a watercolour by R. Knotel. They wear the distinctive four-sided Polish-style *chapska* helmet.

70

A lancer of the Belgian Guides Corps passing French infantry in 1914. He is also armed with a carbine and wears a drab cloth cover over his traditional *chapska*.

In 1811 Napoleon – impressed, so it is said, by the performance of a body of Polish lancers in his service – converted six regiments of dragoons into lancers. They often proved useful when attacking infantry squares or formations, for their long weapons outreached the musket and fixed bayonet of the foot soldiers. Lancers were ruthlessly effective when pursuing a fleeing enemy. French *lanciers* were also armed with sword, pistols and carbine. In 1816 four light dragoon regiments of the British army were designated lancers and armed with ash-shafted weapons 16 feet long; later reduced in length to a more manageable 9 feet and the ash pole replaced by bamboo.

Although lancer regiments were popular with many armies the lance itself was a difficult weapon to handle effectively and in the British army, in particular, its use was always controversial. Some considered it the

71

'queen of weapons' while others thought it should be dispensed with in favour of the sword. Captain Louis Nolan of the 15th Hussars (the man who delivered the order that launched the ill-fated Charge of the Light Brigade at Balaclava) had very little regard for the lance and in his book *Cavalry: Its History and Tactics*, published in 1853, had this to say:

'If lances be such good weapons, surely those who wield them ought to acquire great confidence in them, whereas it is well-known that, in battle, lancers generally throw them away, and take to their swords. I never spoke with an English lancer who had been engaged in the late Sikh wars that did not declare the lance to be a useless tool, and a great incumbrance in close conflict.'

Nevertheless, the lance in the hands of a well-trained trooper was an effective weapon for shock impact and instrument of pursuit. The British 17th Lancers used the weapon to cruel and efficient purpose in smashing the mighty Zulu army at Ulundi on 4 July 1879. The British column, some 5,000 strong, under Lord Chelmsford found itself surrounded by an estimated 20,000 Zulu warriors. The British formed a square with the cavalry in the centre. The Zulus attacked and were repulsed by heavy fire from guns, rifles, and Gatling machine guns. Prevented from getting to close quarters the Zulus wavered and seemed to lose heart. At this point Chelmsford let loose the 17th Lancers under Colonel Drury Lowe. 'Go at them, Lowe,' ordered Chelmsford, 'but don't pursue too far.'

A roaring cheer burst from the infantry square as the 17th – nicknamed the 'Death or Glory Boys' – swept out and with lowered lances charged the enemy, who stood firm and opened fire with rifles and muskets, emptying many saddles. 'A moment more,' runs the graphic description in the *Story of the Zulu Campaign*:

Drawn by J. H. Thornely.

A LANCER AT THE "CHARGE."

A lancer at the 'Charge' during the Boer War of 1899-1902, drawn by J. H. Thornely. The lance was finally abolished in the British army in 1927.

'and the bristling line of steel meets the black and shining wall of human flesh, rent, pierced, and gashed, by a weapon as death-dealing and unsparing as their own *assegai* [short stabbing spear]. Still, though crushed and stabbed by the lances, and though their fierce army was scattered like sea-foam, the zulus fought in stubborn knots, nor cried for quarter, stabbing at the horse bellies as they went down, and trying to drag the men off them in the melee. The lance was now relegated in most instances to its sling, and the heavy sabres of the troopers became red with gore.'

The hitherto victorious Zulu army broke and scattered in every direction, the lancers being joined in the two-mile pursuit by a troop of the King's Dragoon Guards and mounted riflemen of the Flying Column under Lieutenant Colonel Buller. The Zulus left some 1,500 dead on the field of Ulundi, a defeat that ended their military power. And a victory that seemed to vindicate the use of the lance. The weapon was retained and used in action by the British in the Boer War at the turn of the century, and also saw active service with the British, French, German and other armies in World War 1.

3 · DEATH OR GLORY!

With the coming of the 19th century the cavalry of Western Europe blossomed into full flower. The Napoleonic Wars saw most of Europe in arms and the uniforms of this period, especially those of the cavalry, were the most flamboyant and colourful in the entire history of military dress. And the 'cavalry spirit' was never more extravagant and pervasive. 'A hussar who is not dead by 30 is a blackguard', was the opinion of the Comte de Lasalle, one of Napoleon's most dashing and reckless cavalry leaders. He was killed by a bullet through the head at the age of 34 in the battle of Wagram in 1809.

In the middle of the century the British cavalry rode into battle against the Russians in the Crimean War attired in all the brilliance of parade ground scarlet and gold: a war of drawing-room glory paid for with great expense of flesh and blood, and notable for the ill-fated Charge of the Light Brigade at Balaclava – a command blunder carried through to the bitter end with disciplined courage.

> 'Half a league, half a league,
> Half a league onward,
> All in the valley of death
> Rode the Six Hundred...
>
> 'Came through the jaws of Death,
> Back from the mouth of Hell,
> All that was left of them,
> Left of Six Hundred...
>
> 'When can their glory fade?
> O the wild charge they made,
> All the world wondered.
> Honour the charge they made,
> Honour the Light Brigade,
> Noble Six Hundred!

Joachim Murat, Marshal of France, one of Napoleon's finest cavalry leaders.

In the Franco-Prussian War of 1870–71 both sides fielded cavalry *en masse* in uniforms little different from those seen at Waterloo. And a Prussian cavalry brigade rode gallantly into the 'jaws of death' during the battle of Mars-la-Tour, a charge known in German history as the *Todtenritt*, the Death Ride. At the century's end the British cavalry, having discarded bright colours for campaign khaki, were still charging 'death or glory' style

at Omdurman against the Dervish army in 1898. And the cavalry spirit, its *raison d'être*, continued to be nurtured and advocated by former cavalrymen in high command well into the 20th century.

The Napoleonic Wars produced a number of celebrated cavalry leaders and cavalry actions: Kellerman at Marengo in 1800, Prince Murat at Jena in 1806 and Eylau in 1807, John Le Marchant at Salamanca in 1812, Von Bock and the King's German Legion at Garcia Hernandez in 1812, and Henry Paget, Earl of Uxbridge, who commanded Wellington's cavalry at Waterloo. Kellerman's charges at Marengo snatched victory from impending defeat for Napoleon. François-Etienne Kellerman, born in 1770, was the son of a cavalry officer who became a Marshal of France. At 15 Kellerman joined his father's hussars' regiment; by the time he was 30 he had reached the rank of brigadier-general.

The battle of Marengo, in northern Italy, was fought between Napoleon and the Austrians to decide mastery over Italy. It began with the Austrians taking the French by surprise in the early morning of 14 June 1800. The Austrian army, 30,000 strong, of which 7,000 were cavalry, was commanded by Baron Melas. By noon the French, inferior in numbers, were in retreat. Part of the Austrian cavalry was deployed in preparation to charge

THE OLD SAUCY
SEVENTH,
Or Queen's Own Regt. of
Lt. Dragoons.

COMMANDED BY THAT GALLANT AND WELL KNOWN HERO,

Lieut. General
HENRY LORD PAGET.

YOUNG Fellows whose hearts beat high to tread the paths of Glory, could not have a better opportunity than now offers. Come forward then, and Enrol yourselves in a Regiment that stands unrivalled, and where the kind treatment, the Men ever experienced is well known throughout the whole Kingdom.

Each Young Hero on being approved, will receive the largest Bounty allowed by Government.

A few smart Young Lads, will be taken at Sixteen Years of Age, 5 Feet 2 Inches, but they must be active, and well limbed. Apply to SERJEANT HOOPER, at

N. B. This Regiment is mounted on Blood Horses, and being lately returned from SPAIN, and the Horses Young, the Men will not be allowed to HUNT during the next Season, more than once a week.

BOOTH AND WRIGHT PRINTERS, NORWICH.

and rout the withdrawing enemy foot soldiers. To prevent this, Kellerman, in command of the cavalry brigade, led the 8th Dragoons (some 300 sabres) in a spirited charge that struck the enemy flank, throwing the Austrian horsemen into confused retreat.

Kellerman's prompt and successful action had won a respite for Napoleon and his hard-pressed army. Napoleon, hanging on desperately at Marengo, was expecting General Desaix to come to his assistance. By early afternoon the Austrians seemed assured of victory. Baron Melas departed the field (he was old and exhausted by the battle), leaving General Zach to finish off the retreating French, who had lost all their guns. At 4 o'clock in the afternoon Desaix made a dramatic appearance, alone, having raced to the field on horse ahead of his fast-approaching army. His appearance put new heart into the French. But he was shot dead leading the infantry in the first counterattack, and the French began to waver and fall back. Napoleon now considered the battle lost.

Again Kellerman saved the situation. As the Austrian grenadiers rushed

77

forward with bayonets fixed at the retreating French infantry, Kellerman, positioned on the right flank, acted without hesitation or consultation, leading his horsemen against the seemingly victorious enemy foot soldiers. Kellerman's charge destroyed three battalions of grenadiers and captured General Zach and two standards. As Kellerman re-formed his 200 survivors, an enemy cavalry regiment came to the aid of the shattered infantry. Yet again Kellerman charged the approaching Austrian horse and hacked them into disorder and retreat, throwing them back into the infantry, causing great confusion.

Instead of allowing his men to pursue the enemy pell-mell and become fragmented as a force, Kellerman managed to keep tight control over his excited horsemen. In this he displayed admirable 'cavalry sense', the lack of which in others brought disastrous results, as we shall see later. He rode to where Napoleon, surrounded by his mounted Consular Guard, was waiting and requested that he be given command of the Guard to reinforce his depleted brigade. Napoleon agreed and Kellerman launched his final attack against the reserve regiments of enemy horse. Without Zach in

An encounter between British and French dragoons at Salamanca 22 July 1812 during the Peninsular campaign. Painted by B. Granville Baker.

78

The Magdeburg Hussar regiment, Prussia, 1800.

command the Austrians began to lose determination. Kellerman's pounding, slashing cavalry finally broke the enemy's morale and the Austrians fled in panic. Next day a treaty was signed between Melas and Napoleon; the latter obtained 12 strong fortresses and became master of north Italy.

Kellerman's quick assessment of a critical situation and his perfect timing had won the day: a few minutes earlier or later and his charges would not have succeeded. 'Time is the great element in all battles,' wrote Field

Sir James Yorke Scarlett, 55 years of age and untried in battle, leads the Heavy Brigade against the Russians at Balaclava and puts them to flight.

Marshal Wolseley, 'but with cavalry minutes are nearly as important as hours are to infantry.' Kellerman, however, received little acknowledgement from Napoleon. 'Kellerman made a lucky charge just at the right moment,' he commented to his aide-de-camp, Bourrienne; 'See what trifling circumstances decide these affairs.' Napoleon disliked Kellerman's arrogance. 'It was I who placed the crown on that man's head,' Kellerman had written in a letter that came to Napoleon's notice. Later, when his wayward conduct caused him to come before Bonaparte, the Emperor chastised but did not punish him, saying: 'Kellerman, whenever your name is brought to my attention, I can remember nothing but Marengo!'

Joachim Murat, Prince Murat, King of Naples, Marshal of France, was the *beau ideal* of the French light cavalry officer – a dashing, brightly uniformed fiery Gascon, a duelling womaniser, a fearless commander who led his horsemen with superb *elan*. In a period of dazzling uniforms, Murat out-dazzled them all with his self-designed outfits. Albrecht Adam in *Memoirs of a War Artist* recalls an incident in Russia in 1812:

'I witnessed the constant coming and going of the emperor's marshals on the banks of the river Duna. It was there I had an amusing experience. I noticed a figure dressed in sky-blue coat covered in gold lace, with gold-laced scarlet trousers, and wearing a curious hat covered with plumes; in other words, a figure which I could not place. Strangest of all was that he kept walking about very near the Emperor... Finally, I approached an officer standing near me. "Tell me," I asked, "who is that extraordinary drum major in whom His Majesty is so interested?" "*Mon Dieu!*" replied the officer – "that is Murat, King of Naples!"'

Born the son of an innkeeper in 1767, Murat joined the cavalry at the age of 20 and 6 years later was made Napoleon's chief aide-de-camp with the

The successful charge of the Heavy Brigade at Balaclava, showing the 6th Inniskilling Dragoons in action. Note the absence of helmet plumes when on active service.

rank of colonel. He distinguished himself in a number of battles. In 1800 he married Caroline Bonaparte, thus becoming Napoleon's brother-in-law. Later Napoleon made him a Marshal of France and a prince. Murat was not a great commander in the sense of tactics and strategy. His great value as a leader lay in the magical manner he could inspire his horsemen, even when they were exhausted, to follow him into the 'jaws of death'.

Murat's finest hour came at Eylau, 7-8 February 1807, when Napoleon saw the battle going badly against the Russians. He called for Murat and said to him, 'Are you going to allow these people to devour us?' He then ordered a grand charge by all his cavalry at the Russian centre. Leading 80 squadrons, the dashing dandy covered 2,500 yards and penetrated the massed ranks of enemy infantry. Two lines were utterly broken, the third falling back. Colonel Lepic and his horse grenadiers of the Imperial Guard overran infantry and artillery and penetrated so far behind the enemy lines that they had to mount another charge at the enemy rear in order to reach the rest of the French cavalry. Murat had removed the pressure and redressed the balance of power. It was an indecisive battle. Both armies withdrew to winter quarters. Murat crowned his spectacular career by accepting the vacant throne of Naples in 1808. In order to retain his throne he schemed against Napoleon, who rejected him. In the end, he had to fight on his own behalf in defence of his crown; he was defeated, taken prisoner, and died bravely before a firing squad in 1815.

The 1st (Royal) Dragoons in 1815. Painted by Richard Simkin.

Waterloo painted by H. Chartier, depicting the moment when the Union Brigade penetrated too far into the enemy ground and were counterattacked by fresh cavalry.

Henry Paget was a remarkable leader of British cavalry with a long and distinguished career embracing active service in Flanders, Holland, the Peninsular War and Waterloo. Born the eldest son of the first Earl of Uxbridge in 1786, he started his military life proper at the age of 24 with the command of a foot regiment he had raised himself. In 1797 he purchased command of the 7th Light Dragoons (later converted to Hussars) and made it one of the most efficient regiments in the army. In 1808 Paget was in command of the cavalry under Sir John Moore in the Peninsular campaign. At Sahagun in Spain, 21 December 1808, Paget led a single cavalry regiment in what Sir Charles Oman in his *A History of the Peninsular War* described as 'perhaps the most brilliant exploit of the British cavalry during the whole six years of the war'.

Lord Paget, intent on driving a strong French force out of Sahagun, set out with the 10th and 15th Hussars, instructing General Slade, with the 10th, to approach the town from one direction while he, leading the 15th,

approached from another. Slade was a slow and cautious man and the 10th failed to take up position on time. Paget with about 350 sabres found himself confronted, 400 yards away, by some 700 enemy dragoons and chasseurs. Paget's declared opinion of a good cavalry commander was that he should 'inspire his men with the most perfect confidence in his personal gallantry. Let him lead, they are sure to follow, and I believe hardly anything will stop them.' Paget acted out precisely that tenet.

He led his yelling hussars in a furious charge that crashed upon the static French with terrible effect. Just before the collision took place a loud cry of surprise and terror arose from the ranks of the French. After a short struggle the French horsemen broke and fled. Paget's hussars pursued them, sabres slashing and thrusting with little pity. In quick time the 15th had smashed two regiments completely (only 200 French escaped death or capture) with losses of two hussars killed and 23 wounded. Among the prisoners were the two commanding colonels of the regiments. When asked why they had received the charge at the halt, they replied that they were quite unaware that there were any British Hussar regiments in the area. They thought the 15th were Spaniards, who never charged home – and realised their mistake too late, hence their loud cry of surprise. We shall meet Lord Paget again, at Waterloo.

The Peninsular War produced another British cavalry commander hero: General John Le Marchant. In the battle of Salamanca, 22 July 1812, the Duke of Wellington defeated the French army of Marshal Marmont. Wellington always regarded Salamanca, Vittoria, and Waterloo as his three finest victories. Salamanca showed the Iron Duke at his best, especially his prompt detection of the enemy's mistakes, and his skill in turning them to his own advantage. 'Marmont wished to cut me off,' he said. 'I saw that in attempting this he was spreading himself over more ground than he could defend. I resolved to attack him, and succeeded in my object very quickly. One of the French generals said I had beaten 40,000 men in 40 minutes.' A colourful phrase but somewhat of an exaggeration: the battle lasted six hours.

Exploiting Marmont's mistake, Wellington attacked with his infantry and broke the enemy position. Now came the time for the British cavalry to throw its considerable weight into the fight and thus make certain of complete victory. Wellington ordered Le Marchant to attack with his heavy brigade. John Le Marchant was born in Guernsey, the Channel Island, in 1766. He began his army career in a foot regiment, transferred to the 2nd Dragoon Guards and later obtained a lieutenant-colonelcy in the 7th Light Dragoons. A serious student of the profession of arms, he introduced a new, more efficient type of cavalry sword and an improved system of sword-exercise. Le Marchant was the first Lieutenant-Governor of the Royal Military College.

At Salamanca Le Marchant commanded the Heavy Cavalry Brigade comprised of dragoons and dragoon guards, some 1,000 sabres. The 'heavies' charged through the thick gun smoke and crashed into the dis-

CAPTAIN NOLAN.

Captain Louis Edward Nolan, 15th Hussars, who delivered the written order that launched the charge of the Light Brigade.

84

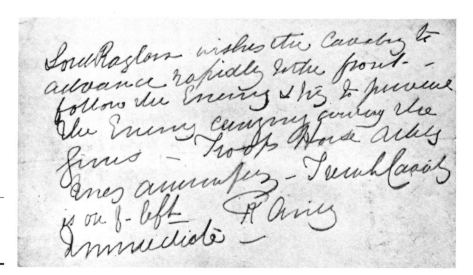

The original order that set the Light Brigade in motion, written down on Raglan's instruction by General Richard Airey and signed by Airey.

ordered enemy ranks: 1,200 French infantry, though formed in several lines, were trampled down with a terrible clamour. Bewildered and blinded, the French foot soldiers cast away their arms and ran through the openings of the British squadrons, crouching and pleading for quarter – while the dragoons, big men on big horses, careered onwards, cutting and thrusting in a dreadful blood lust.

The 'heavies' struck first the 66th Regiment, which was formed in a sort of column of half battalions, thus presenting six successive lines which broke into a heavy musketry fire as the cavalry dashed upon their front. Over these the 'heavies' rode at the gallop, simply trampling them out of the fight.

A second French battalion of 600 men was likewise crushed under pounding hooves and whirling blades. Onward swept the battle-mad horsemen. By this time the open trees, under which the 'heavies' were riding, were growing closer and the front of the charging line was greatly broken. A solid French brigade, which stood in the shelter of the trees, poured a volley into the galloping squadrons and scores of saddles were emptied. Yet Le Marchant's juggernaut rolled on and crushed this brigade also. Lord Edward Somerset, with a single squadron, seeing beyond him a battery of five guns, pushed on his attack and captured them.

This history-shaking charge destroyed three French divisions, and captured five guns, two eagle standards, and 7,000 prisoners. The Heavy Brigade suffered losses of 105 – including Major General John Le Marchant, shot dead leading his men.

The day after Salamanca, a remarkable event in the story of cavalry took place at Garcia Hernandez: horsemen actually broke and destroyed a French infantry square of steady ranks fully prepared to receive a charge. Throughout the 19th century it was virtually impossible for cavalry to break such a square, especially a British square, of disciplined, determined foot soldiers armed with musket and bayonet. It happened at Garcia

Hernandez by accident. In pursuit of the retreating French, Wellington sent the 1st and 2nd Dragoons of the King's German Legion commanded by Major-General von Bock.

The Legion came into being in 1804, its ranks filled with Hanoverians loyal to George III, who as King of England was also Elector of Hanover. When Britain went to war with Napoleon in 1803, Napoleon invaded Hanover, disbanded its army, and plundered the land. Hundreds of Hanoverian soldiers made their way to England and the King's German Legion was raised (5,000 strong including cavalry, artillery and infantry) to fight under British command against the hated Napoleon. Its cavalry consisted of two regiments of dragoons and three of hussars, dressed in uniforms similar to their British counterparts. The Legion proved 'Brave and True' – *Tapfer und Treu* (motto of the 1st Dragoons) in the heat of battle and was never found wanting in soldierly conduct.

At Garcia Hernandez, von Bock and a brigade of heavy dragoons found themselves in a valley confronted by the French rearguard deployed in solid infantry squares. Von Bock launched his horsemen. The left squadron, commanded by Captain von der Decken, wheeled into line and charged the nearest square, to be met by volley after volley: the two front ranks of the square kneeling, presenting a double row of steel bayonets; standing above them, four ranks deep, their comrades fired steadily at the

Corporal John Shaw, 2nd Life Guards, distinguished himself at Waterloo but did not survive the battle.

Sergeant Ewart of the Scots Greys captured the eagle standard of the 45th Regiment at Waterloo and returned home a national hero.

86

James Thomas Brudenell, Seventh Earl of Cardigan, the small-minded martinet who led the charge of the Light Brigade with unflinching courage.

fast approaching mass of cavalry. The Germans pushed their assault up to the very points of the bayonets. They enveloped the square but could not break it. Von der Decken was among the first to fall.

When it seemed that the dragoons were about to withdraw, a shot killed a barging horse that fell with its rider on to the square, causing a gap in the defence, through which the dragoons lost no time in spurring through their terrified and kicking mounts. The dead horse, as John Keegan points out in his *The Face of Battle*, 'had done what living flesh and blood could not: act as a giant projectile to batter a hole in the face of the square'.

Lieutenant Alexander Dunn, 11th Hussars, won the Victoria Cross during the charge of the Light Brigade by riding to the rescue of an unhorsed comrade who was under close attack.

Meanwhile another squadron under Captain von Reitzeuslen charged fiercely at the second French square positioned on higher ground. The French, having witnessed the destruction of the first square, were nervous to the point of breaking. Several men deserted the square and ran for their lives. The hurricane of horses and deadly steel swept over the weakened square and scattered its members in a welter of blood and German curses. A third square was also overwhelmed. The dragoons took 1,400 prisoners, with a loss to themselves of more than 100 dead and wounded. Wellington was full of praise for the exploit:

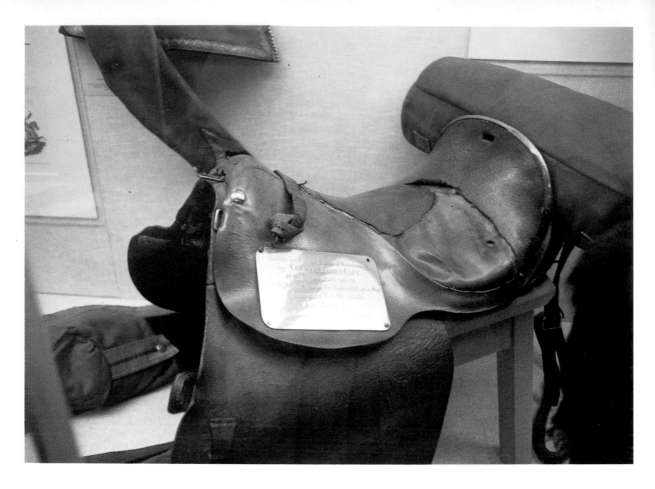

'I have never witnessed a more gallant charge than was made upon the enemy's infantry by the heavy brigade of the King's German Legion under Major-General von Bock, which was completely successful, and the whole body of infantry, consisting of three battalions of the enemy's first divisions, were made prisoners.'

The King's German Legion also served under Wellington at Waterloo in June 1815. So did Henry Paget (of Sahagun fame) who, now Lieutenant-General the Earl of Uxbridge, commanded the cavalry in Wellington's Anglo-Allied army of 68,000 on the day of battle. 'It was,' in Uxbridge's view, 'the prettiest field day of cavalry and horse artillery that I ever witnessed.' It was also a day of stoic heroism and great suffering and death. The battle of Waterloo was a complex one and, perforce, must be dealt with here in a simplified manner with the emphasis on the cavalry actions, of which the Union Brigade figures chiefly.

Waterloo was the first and only time that Napoleon and Wellington directly faced each other as opposing commanders. Napoleon, fielding 72,000 men, was confident of victory. 'Tonight,' he told his staff officers, 'we shall sleep in Brussels.' Wellington, with 68,000 men, had prepared himself for a hard slogging match and hoped that Marshal Blucher – who

The saddle used by Lieutenant James Gape, Scots Greys, at Waterloo. During the charge of the Union Brigade his saddle was twice pierced by bullets, one through the pommel and one through the back of the seat. His horse had three slight wounds but he himself was unscathed. The saddle can be seen at Edinburgh Castle.

90

Spanish lancers of 1835.

had re-formed his Prussian army after his defeat at Ligny – would arrive in proper time to help him. Napoleon had some 11,000 cavalry; the Iron Duke's horsemen totalled about 12,000 of which some 7,000 were British.

The battle began about 11.30 am on the morning of 18 June. Napoleon opened with massed cannon fire and then directed a strong attack on Wellington's right flank, which was guarded by the fortified chateau of Hougomont. After several hours of hard fighting the French were repulsed at Hougomont and Napoleon launched his main attack at Wellington's centre. With drums beating the *pas de charge* and with repeated shouts of *'Vive l'Empéreur!'* the dense mass of blue-coated infantry supported by cavalry burst upon the Allied lines. They smashed through the Dutch-Belgian brigade and advanced on the red-coated British infantry.

Lieutenant-General Sir Thomas Picton's infantry division stood firm and halted the enemy's advances. Picton led a counterattack and was killed. At this critical moment Lord Uxbridge, clearly recognising the dangerous situation, ordered the Household Brigade and the Union Brigade of heavy cavalry to charge the advancing enemy. The Household Brigade, commanded by Major-General Lord Edward Somerset, consisted of the 1st and 2nd Life Guards, the Royal Horse Guards (the Blues), and the 1st Dragoon

Guards. The Union Brigade, so called because it consisted of an English, a Scots and an Irish regiment, was commanded by Major-General Sir William Ponsonby and composed of the 1st Royal Dragoons, 2nd Dragoons (the Scots Greys), and 6th Inniskilling Dragoons.

Uxbridge sent the Union Brigade against the infantry, while he led the Household Brigade against the supporting French cuirassiers. With the advantage of a descending slope, and riding fresh horses over a shorter distance than the enemy, the Household Brigade collided with the French horsemen 'like two walls, in the most perfect lines,' in the words of an eyewitness. The two brigades fused in a flailing of sabres. Corporal John Shaw of the 2nd Life Guards distinguished himself that day by his herculean strength and valour. A prominent prizefighter, Shaw slew nine of the enemy in single combat before breaking his sword and falling victim to a number of French blades. The cuirassiers, well beaten, turned and fled with the guardsmen in hot pursuit.

The Union Brigade was just as successful in overwhelming the enemy. Napoleon, who witnessed the devastation wrought by the Scots Greys (on grey mounts) is said to have remarked: 'Les terribles chevaux gris.' Sergeant Ewart of the Greys captured an eagle standard of the 45th

'All That was Left of Them, Left of Six Hundred', from the painting by R. Caton Woodville, showing the roll-call after the charge.

93

Regiment and received a commission, and much celebrity for his valour. He described the incident himself:

'I had a hard contest for it. The [standard] bearer thrust for my groin [with his bayonet]; I parried it off and cut him through the head. After which I was attacked by one of their lancers, who threw his lance at me, but missed the mark by my throwing it off with my sword. Then I cut him from the chin upwards, which went through his teeth. Next I was attacked by a foot soldier, who after firing at me charged me with his bayonet; but he very soon lost the combat, for I parried it and cut him down through the head, so that finished the contest for the eagle.'

Not found wanting in aggressive courage, the British cavalry were, however, sadly lacking in discipline and sound military sense. The madness of battle prevailed: seeing the enemy flee before them inflamed the triumphant soldiers to pursue and kill. The Union Brigade charged too far into enemy ground, into the enemy guns and beyond and found themselves broken into scattered groups with no cohesion. When the French counterattacked with fresh cavalry, the Union Brigade, its ranks

94

Looking down into the 'valley of death' as the brilliant ranks of the Light Brigade gallop to disaster against the guns.

decimated and horses blown by the long ride, was badly cut up. The Scots Greys started out with 416 men and suffered 200 men and 224 horses killed or wounded.

Such unbridled rashness lost Wellington a quarter of his entire cavalry. Some years later he said 'I considered our cavalry inferior to the French from want of order... They [the British] could gallop, but could not preserve order.' General Excelmann, one of Napoleon's best cavalry leaders, had this to say after Waterloo:

'Your horses are the finest in the world and your men ride better than any Continental soldier. With such material the English cavalry ought to have done more than has ever been accomplished by them on the field of battle. The great deficiency is in your officers who seem to be impressed by the conviction that they can dash or ride after everything, as if the art of war were precisely the same as that of fox hunting.'

It must be said that as soon as the regimental commanders saw their men running out of control they sounded the rally but, as Uxbridge commented, 'neither voice nor trumpet availed'. Sir William Ponsonby rode forward in an attempt to arrest the wild career of his men, only to find himself on an exhausted horse that could move no faster than a walk. He and his aide-de-camp were speared to death by the ruthless lancers of Jacquinot's cavalry division.

The 12th Light Dragoons, commanded by Colonel Frederick Ponsonby, was part of Sir John Vandeleur's brigade sent in to bring out survivors of

Four survivors of the charge of the Light Brigade photographed in 1856. Left to right: Corporal Thomas Smith, Corporal William Dimmock, Private William Pearson, Corporal Thomas Foster. All of the 17th Lancers.

Another proud survivor of the Light Brigade charge: Cornet John Wilkin, 11th Hussars, who posed for photographer Roger Fenton in the camp at Balaclava.

the Union Brigade. The light dragoons dashed through a body of French horse, then ran into a fresh regiment of Polish lancers. Ponsonby relates the manner in which he was severely wounded:

'In the melee I was almost instantly disabled in both arms, losing first my sword, and then my reins, and followed by a few men, who were presently cut down, no quarter being allowed, asked, or given. I was carried along by my horse, till, receiving a blow from a sabre, I fell senseless on my face to the ground. Recovering, I raised myself a little to look round, being at that time, I believe, in a condition to get up and run away – when a lancer passing by cried out "*Tu n'est pas mort, coquin!*" and stuck his lance through my back. My head dropped, the blood gushed into my mouth, a difficulty of breathing came on, and I thought all was over.'

It has been written that the French at Waterloo suffered more, perhaps, from the want of able cavalry leaders than from anything else. Of all Napoleon's generals only Kellerman was a cavalry leader of note. Murat would have proved invaluable that day and Napoleon bitterly regretted later that he had rejected him. 'Murat' he wrote 'would perhaps have achieved victory for us.' Marshal Ney, who led the cavalry as well as the infantry charges at Waterloo was (no matter how brave, how much experienced in war) a poor substitute for Murat, who had the charisma to inspire his men with the utmost devotion and his enemies with great fear.

Ney made matters worse by disregarding the advice of Kellerman, a superior leader of horse. Time and again Ney (who had five mounts killed under him) led massed cavalry charges that were repulsed by artillery and infantry squares. At about 4 pm Ney committed all his cavalry to a grand attack. Kellerman implored him to keep part of his immense force, some 10,000 strong, in reserve but Ney remained obdurate. Napoleon considered this charge premature. 'Ney is too early by an hour!' he exclaimed. One

Charge of the Chasseurs d'Afrique, October 25.

While the Light Brigade charged in the valley the French 4th Chasseurs d'Afrique attacked and silenced the enemy guns on the Fedioukine Heights, therefore lessening the casualties suffered by the Light Brigade.

account tells us that 'Every arm of the mounted service was represented in this attack, the beauty and brilliancy of the uniforms baffling description.'

This assault, said to be the greatest mass assault by cavalry against infantry, proved no more successful than the previous efforts.

'For upwards of an hour our squares were surrounded by the elite of the French cavalry,' wrote Lord Hill, commander of the 2nd Corps. 'They gallantly stood within forty paces of us, unable to leap over the bristling line of bayonets, unwilling to retire, and determined never to surrender. Hundreds of them were dropping in all directions from our murderous fire, yet as fast as they dropped others came up to supply their places.'

General Foy of the French army paid tribute to the stalwart redcoats: 'Neither the bullets of the Imperial Guard nor the hitherto victorious French cavalry could break the immovable British infantry. One would have been inclined to believe that they had taken root to the ground.' Twelve times between 4 and 6 pm Ney led or sent forward the cavalry against the squares. In vain the horsemen cut desperately at the hedge of bayonets; in vain they trotted up and fired pistols at the squares.

The arrival of Blucher and his Prussians on the field made an Allied victory certain and complete. At about 8 pm Wellington ordered the whole line to advance in pursuit of the fleeing French. At last the great slaughter

came to an end: the French lost some 30,000 men of whom 7,000 were captured; Wellington lost 15,000 men and Blucher 7,000. After the battle Wellington wrote a letter expressing his sadness at his heavy casualties:

'My heart is broken by the terrible loss I have sustained in my old friends and companions, and my poor soldiers. Believe me, nothing except a battle lost, can be half so melancholy as a battle won; the bravery of my troops has hitherto saved me from the greater evil; but to win such a battle as this of Waterloo, at the expense of so many gallant friends, could only be termed a heavy misfortune but for the result to the public.'

The mangled and mutilated were eventually gathered up, horses were put down, the wounded soldiers died or survived. Those who survived received the Waterloo Medal. Many veterans of the mass carnage were crippled and maimed for life and died in poverty. Nevertheless there must have been very few veterans of that monumental battle who did not feel proud to say 'I served at Waterloo.'

Lord Cardigan was the first into and over the guns. He came through the encounter with a slight lance wound and a great deal of glory. Painting by T. Jones Barker.

98

A monument in Cardiff, Wales, to a Light Brigade hero: Godfrey First Viscount Tredegar, who in the charge, as Captain Godfrey Charles Morgan, led a troop of the 17th Lancers.

The most celebrated cavalry action of the Crimean War was the Charge of the Light Brigade on 25 October 1854, in which some 600 British horsemen made an heroic but foolhardy frontal attack on Russian field guns, at the same time running a gauntlet of fire from enemy guns positioned on the flanks. It was a shocking waste of brave men and horses, who went without question into the 'mouth of hell' because of a misinterpreted order – an incident that seems to bring into sharp focus the entire political and military mismanagement of the war. Lord Tennyson dramatised the death ride in ringing stanzas that assured its lasting fame.

> '"Forward, the Light Brigade!"
> Was there a man dismayed?
> Not though the soldier knew
> Someone had blundered:
> Their's not to make reply,
> Their's not to reason why,
> Their's but to do and die:
> Into the valley of Death
> Rode the Six Hundred.'

It is not generally appreciated that the folly of the Light Brigade was preceded on the same day by another British cavalry charge – that of the Heavy Brigade – which has been described as one of the most desperate and decisive cavalry versus cavalry actions in history. Tennyson's panegyric effort on behalf of the Heavy Brigade (300 strong) did not reach the same poetic quality and popular appeal as that of the 'Noble Six Hundred'.

On 25 October 1854 a huge Russian army marched against the small sea port of Balaclava, through which the Allied army (British, French and Turkish) was being supplied. The battle of Balaclava developed into three distinct actions. First came the gallant stand of the 93rd Highlanders who defended the valley leading down to the harbour. The Highlanders – the 'Thin Red Line' – only 550 strong, stood firm, without cavalry or artillery support, and repulsed a large force of enemy cavalry and horse artillery. Lord Raglan, the British commander, ordered the Heavy Brigade to support the Highlanders. The brigade, commanded by Sir James Yorke Scarlett, consisted of the 4th and 5th Dragoon Guards, the Royal Dragoons, the Scots Greys, and the 6th Inniskilling Dragoons.

As the brigade moved across the valley into support, Scarlett's attention was capture by the sudden appearance of Russian cavalry on the ridge above to his left, and descending *en masse*. On this occasion Scarlett certainly cut to pieces the military dictum that 'Cavalry should be composed of young men; an old man, as a rule, is out of place in its ranks, either as an officer or as a private. It requires the dash and fire of youth; age brings caution and with it hesitation.' Scarlett was a white-whiskered 55 years old who had never heard a shot fired in anger. Yet he did not hesitate in his decision to charge the enemy mass, nor was he lacking in dash and fire.

'Left wheel into line!' he commanded and the leading squadrons of the Heavy Brigade, two of Greys and one of Inniskillings, swung into line to

General von Bredow, distinguished cavalry officer who led the Prussian Heavy Brigade against the French guns and infantry at Mars-la-Tour on 16 August 1870.

100

The Prussian 16th Uhlan regiment crashes into the French positions during the celebrated 'Death Ride' at Mars-la-Tour.

face the enemy. This movement was carried out so correctly and with such parade-ground *sangfroid* that the Russians, who had descended the slope and were now some 400 yards from Scarlett's line, halted in hesitation. The British trumpeter sounded the charge and, with its commander in the lead, the Greys and Inniskillings moved into battle at the trot that quickened into a gallop – some 300 sabres against more than 3,000 of the enemy. The rest of the Heavy Brigade, which had been at the rear of the column and had not had time to close up and change direction, joined in a little later. Captain Temple Godman of the 5th Dragoon Guards, which came up in support of the Greys, witnessed the scene as Scarlett's men crashed into the Russian host:

'As soon as they met all I saw were swords in the air in every direction, the pistols going off and everyone hacking away right and left. In a moment the Greys were surrounded and hemmed in. There they were fighting back to back, in the middle, the great bearskin caps high above the enemy. This was the work of a moment. Then the 5th advanced and in they charged yelling and shouting as loud as they could. The row was tremendous and for about five minutes neither would give way, and their column was so deep we could not cut through it. At length they turned. . . and the whole ran as hard as they could back up the hill, our man after them, all broken up, and cutting them right and left. We pursued them about 300 yards and then called off with much difficulty, then gunners opened up on them and gave them a fierce peppering.'

It was a remarkable feat of arms; a small body of horsemen putting to flight enemy cavalry far superior in number. When the Royals and 4th Dragoon

Uniforms of the Chasseurs d'Afrique.

Guards threw in their weight the Russian retreat turned into a rout. The 93rd Highlanders had witnessed the charge and Sir Colin Campbell rode up to the Scots Greys, who had been foremost in the action, and exclaimed: 'Gallant Greys! I am sixty-one years old, but if I were a lad again I would be proud to be in your ranks!' It was also said of Sir Colin that when a captured Russian officer, curious about the Highlanders' kilts, asked him who the fierce soldiers in skirts were, the gruff Scotsman replied, 'The wives of the men on the grey horses.'

As the Russian horsemen retreated in confusion they passed right across

102

the front of the Light Cavalry Brigade, waiting and watching in the North Valley. Had Lord Cardigan, the brigade commander, seized his opportunity and attacked the fleeing enemy the Russians would have been cut to pieces and unable, as they did, to re-form behind their artillery at the end of the valley. But Lord Cardigan had his orders from Lord Lucan, commanding the Cavalry Division, 'to stay in your position, on no account leave it, and defend it against any attack.' Cardigan so little understood his business as a soldier that he assumed that the order to defend prohibited him from the attack. Lucan later refuted Cardigan's interpretation, saying he had told him to attack anything within reach of his position. Cardigan and Lucan were brothers-in-law and detested each other. Appointing one Commander of the Cavalry Division and the other Commander of the Light Brigade was an act of folly committed by the War Office.

James Thomas Brudenell, Seventh Earl of Cardigan, was 57 years old, a martinet and parade-ground soldier, a stickler for military etiquette and dress. His mind was narrow and inflexible, although his physical courage was never in doubt. A man of great wealth, he purchased his way up the ladder of military promotion and in 1836 became the commander of the 11th Light Dragoons. He lavished his own money on the regiment, making it one of the smartest in the army. In 1840 the regiment was chosen to

escort Prince Albert of Saxe-Coburg on his arrival in England to marry Queen Victoria. The prince was so impressed with the regiment's turn-out that he requested that it be made his own. Consequently the Queen directed that 'the 11th Regiment of Light Dragoons shall be armed, clothed and equipped as Hussars and styled the 11th, or Prince Albert's Own Hussars'. A splendid wedding present!

Cardigan dressed his horsemen in crimson overalls (trousers) and the regiment gained the nickname 'the Cherubims', more rudely referred to as 'the Cherrybums'. They certainly cut a dash, as *The Times* reported: 'The brevity of their jackets, the irrationality of their headgear, the incredible tightness of their cherry-coloured pants, altogether defy description: they must be seen to be appreciated.' At Balaclava the 11th Hussars were somewhat soiled by hard campaigning and primitive camp life; 'soldiers with the gilding off' as William Russell of *The Times* described them. The most brilliant figure in their ranks was Cardigan who, living on his luxury yacht in the harbour, maintained himself in parade ground condition.

George Bingham, Earl of Lucan, purchased command of the 17th Lancers in 1826 and, like his brother-in-law, spent enormous sums of his own money on blood horses and magnificent uniforms for the regiment, earning it the nickname 'Bingham's Dandies'. On their respective appointments in the Crimean War a fellow officer made the comment: 'Cardigan has as much brains as my boot. He is only to be equalled in want of intellect by his relation the Earl of Lucan... two such fools could hardly be picked out of the British Army.' Another 'Cherrybum' wrote: 'We all agree that two greater muffs than Lucan and Cardigan could not be. We call Lucan the cautious ass [nicknamed ''Lord Look-on''] and Cardigan the dangerous ass.'

The final encounter of the day-long cavalry versus cavalry struggle at Mars-la-Tour. In this last engagement some 5,000 horsemen fought it out with sabre, lance and firearms. Illustrated by R. Knotel.

Having lost a splendid opportunity to annihilate the fleeing enemy cavalry, Cardigan awaited further orders. Lord Raglan, the commander-in-chief, from his high viewpoint at one end of the North valley, observed the Russians about to remove guns from several redoubts they had captured on the Causeway Heights, to his right. To prevent this military disgrace, Raglan sent an order (the fourth such order) to Lucan, via Captain Nolan, that read:

'Lord Raglan wishes the Cavalry to advance rapidly to the front – follow the enemy and try to prevent the enemy carrying away the guns – Troop Horse Artillery may accompany – French cavalry is on your left. Immediate.'

Raglan chose Captain Louis Edward Nolan to take the message because this bright young hussar was a most skilful horseman. He descended the heights to the plain some 600 feet below at considerable speed, urged by Raglan's final verbal order: 'Tell Lord Lucan he is to attack immediately.' Nolan was a professional soldier. He had written a book on cavalry tactics; he was talented, ambitious and arrogant, contemptuous of hidebound commanders like Lord Lucan. From his viewpoint, Lucan could see nothing of the guns being taken off. 'Attack what? What guns, sir?' he queried, studying the written order. Nolan, in angry impatience, flung out his arm ambiguously, not pointing to the Causeway Heights, but to the end of the North Valley, where the enemy cavalry now stood behind a line of guns. 'There, my lord, is your enemy, there are your guns!'

Furious at Nolan's taunt, Lucan ordered Cardigan to advance. Cardigan brought down his sword in salute. 'Certainly, sir, but allow me to point out that the Russians have a battery in our front and batteries and riflemen on

'Disabled!' Showing a wounded French dragoon during the Franco-Prussian war. From the painting by P. Grolleron.

both flanks.' Lucan replied: 'I know it, but Lord Raglan will have it. We have no choice but to obey.' Cardigan at once ordered his brigade to advance, making the loud aside, 'Here goes the last of the Brudenells.' The Light Brigade was understrength, having suffered much from sickness, and numbered 673 all ranks. Cardigan rode immaculately at the head of three lines of the finest light cavalry in the world: the 17th Lancers and 13th Light Dragoons formed the first line, the 11th Hussars the second line, the 4th Light Dragoons and 8th Hussars the third.

Lord Lucan followed behind leading the Heavy Brigade. On seeing the awful casualties of the Light Brigade, Lucan decided to withdraw and form a support on which the Light Brigade could retire. The Light Brigade rode at the guns alone. Nolan had joined the charge. But before the brigade had moved a hundred paces he galloped across its front from left to right, shouting and waving his sword. His behaviour mystified and outraged Cardigan. It would seem that Nolan had realised the order had been mis-understood and attempted to correct it. At that moment a shell burst near him and he was killed. Sergeant-Major Loy Smith, 11th Hussars, took part in the charge:

'The trumpets now sounded the advance... As we moved off the Russians opened fire from all their batteries, the round shot passed through us and the shells burst over and amongst us, causing great havoc. The first man of my troop that was struck was Private Young, a cannon ball taking off his right arm, I being close to his right rear, fancied I felt the wind from it as it passed me; I afterwards found I was bespattered with his flesh. To such a nicety were the enemy's guns elevated for our destruction, that before we had advanced many hundreds yards Private Turner's left arm was also struck off close to the shoulder and Private Ward was struck full in the chest, a shell too burst over us, a piece of which struck Cornet Houghton in the forehead and mortally wounded him.'

106

Uniforms of the German Empire, Franco-Prussian War period. Cavalry regiments from the Kingdom of Saxony.

With only a few yards to go, Cardigan quickened his pace to a gallop. The lances of the 17th dropped down to the 'engage'. With the horsemen only 80 yards away, the Russians fired their final salvo. Half the British line went down. But the remainder, Cardigan still leading, crashed through the smoke upon guns and gunners, spearing and sabring. The guns were taken and the Russian cavalry attacked.

After a tremendous struggle the survivors of the Light Brigade either rode, staggered on foot, crawled or were carried back to the protection of the Heavy Brigade. Out of 673 horsemen who started out, 195 mounted men answered the roll call. Of the 17th Lancers and 13th Light Dragoons of the first line, only 35 lancers answered their names, while the 13th could only muster ten men. Some 500 horses were killed in the great slaughter that lasted 20 minutes. Cardigan came through it all with a slight lance wound. Deeply grieved at the reckless ruination of his pride and joy, the Light Brigade, he exclaimed to the survivors at rollcall: 'Men, it is a mad-brained trick, but it is no fault of mine.' He later retired to his yacht to ruminate over a bottle of champagne, while the remnants of his brigade suffered and wondered.

The French General Bosquet, looking down from the heights, summed up the heroic, hapless charge perfectly: 'It is magnificent, but it is not war.' It must be added that the casualties of the Light Brigade would have been greater had not the French commander sent his cavalry – the 4th Chasseurs d'Afrique – to attack and silence the enemy batteries on the

107

A German hussar vedette. A vedette was a mounted sentinel: 'A trooper posted on horseback with his horse's head towards the place whence any danger is to be feared and his carbine advanced, with the butt-end against his right thigh.'

Fedioukine Heights. Recriminations and controversy over the Charge of the Light Brigade continued for many years after the war ended in March 1856, the year in which the Victoria Cross, Britain's highest honour for conspicuous bravery in the presence of the enemy, was instituted. Queen Victoria presided over the first investiture in Hyde Park, 26 June 1857.

Two VCs were awarded to Scots Greys of the Heavy Brigade and seven in the Light Brigade action, all nine being awarded for saving the lives of wounded and dismounted comrades in danger of death. Lieutenant Dunn of the 11th Hussars, having survived the charge into the guns and now on his way back, turned his horse and rode into the 'mouth of Hell' again to rescue Sergeant Bentley, who on foot was under attack by three dragoons. Dunn, a big man and a superb swordsman, slew them all with sabre cuts. He then killed a Russian hussar who was attacking the dismounted Private Levett.

Sixteen years after the Charge of the Light Brigade, German cavalry made a similar death or glory gallop against French artillery, machine-gun fire and infantry in the battle of Mars-la-Tour on 16 August 1870 during the Franco-Prussian War. The German poet Freiligrath immortalised the charge in *The Trumpeter of Mars-la-Tour*:

> 'Death and destruction they belched forth in vain,
> We grimly defied their thunder,
> Two columns of foot and batteries twain —
> We rode and cleft them asunder.

Dragoons of the Austro-Hungarian army in 1892.

'With brandished sabres, with reins all slack,
Raised standards, and low-couched lances,
Thus we Uhlans and Cuirassiers wildly drove back,
And hotly repelled their advances.

'But the ride was a ride of death and of blood;
With our thrusts we forced them to sever,
But of two whole regiments, lusty and good,
Out of two men, one rose never.

'With breast shot through, with brow gaping wide,
They lay pale and cold in the valley,
Snatched away in their youth, in their manhood's pride –
Now, Trumpeter, sound the rally!'

The French and German cavalry of 1870 were little different in appearance and in spirit to the horsemen of Waterloo. Cuirassiers wore breastplate, metal helmet, and carried sabre and firearms. Uhlans were armed with lances, hussars wore bright traditional uniforms. In this war, however, German cavalry had to face the innovation of the French machine-gun: the *mitrailleuse*.

The charge took place when the battle of Mars-la-Tour had reached a crucial point. Ruin or retreat stared the Germans in the face as the French threatened to turn their weakened left flank and take Vionville. The

Germans were expecting reinforcements but these had not yet arrived. Time had to be purchased with blood. An order was sent to General von Bredow to bring forward his heavy cavalry brigade, being held just beyond Vionville, that consisted of the 7th Magdeburg Cuirassiers and the 16th Uhlans.

'That infantry must be broken' von Bredow was told. 'That infantry is supported by artillery and *mitrailleuse,*' parried the general, a distinguished cavalry officer, indicating the folly of horsemen charging guns and unshaken infantry in prepared position. 'The fate of the day depends upon it,' replied the chief of staff. 'General Alvensleben has decided that the heavy cavalry brigade must be sacrificed in order to save the infantry.'

That was reason enough for von Bredow. He quickly formed his brigade into a line of squadrons: the cuirassiers on the left, the uhlans on the right. And away they went, riding boot to boot, straight at the lines of guns and infantry, the latter armed with the best bolt-action breech-loading rifle in Europe. The French also had enfilade fire on both flanks. The Prussian horsemen thundered through the hail of shot and shell and burst upon the first line of guns, sabring and spearing the gunners; then on to the second line of infantry, wreaking equal havoc. Von Bredow's brigade had taken the French somewhat by surprise.

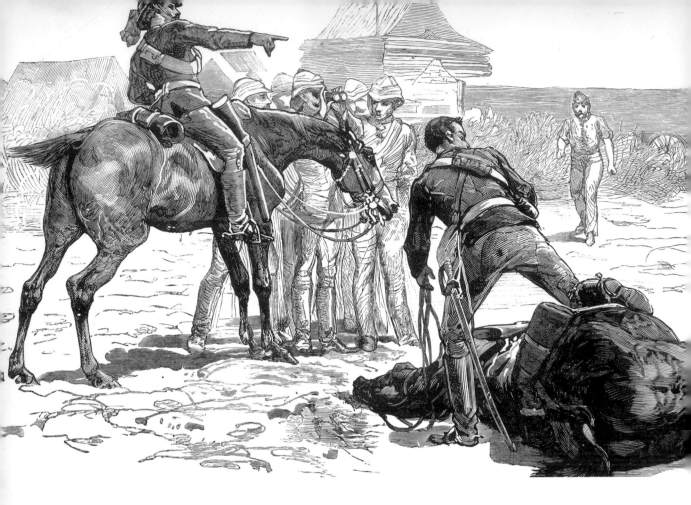

'On taking position with my battery,' said General Henri, 'nothing was to be seen of Prussian cavalry. Where in the world had these cuirassiers come from? All of a sudden they were upon my guns like a whirlwind, and rode or cut down all my men save only me... It was only by the skin of my teeth that I myself escaped as the furious horsemen swept past me, trampling down or sabring the gunners.'

Major Count Schmettow, commanding the 7th Cuirassiers, described the initial impact: 'Every one of the gunners of the first battery were cut down or pierced [the count himself striking down the captain]. In approaching the second battery my helmet was pierced by two bullets and my orderly officer thrown from his horse, wounded in two places.'

In the excitement and the pounding success of their hooves the German brigade, like the Union Brigade at Waterloo, pressed far beyond a prudent distance, and like the British horsemen, paid a terrible price for venturing too far into enemy ground. As the Germans came to the end of their long, arduous gallop just beyond Rezonville, they were set upon in the most ferocious manner by an overwhelming force of French cavalry. The survivors of von Bredow's brigade, exhausted by fighting, their horses blown, now engaged a fresh enemy stronger by five to one. Serving with

Two troopers of the 19th Hussars bring news to Suakim that a reconnoitring force has been cut off by the enemy during the British campaign in Egypt, February 1885. One of the horses has been ridden to exhaustion. From a sketch by a military officer reproduced in *The Graphic*.

Saddlers of the 17th Lancers at work in England in 1896. Four years later the 'Death or Glory Boys' would see hard active service in the Boer War.

the Magdeburg Cuirassiers was a young Scotsman, of whom Count Schmettow wrote:

'Lieutenant Campbell, the Scottish officer, when the French Cuirassiers fell upon us, seized the eagle [standard] of the regiment in his left hand, which was at once shattered by a bullet, and he was surrounded by the French horsemen; but some of our own Cuirassiers cut their way desperately towards him and saved his life.'

Campbell of Craigneish was actually carried out of the battle by Colonel Pemberton, war correspondent of *The Times* who rode with the Prussians as a spectator! After putting up a stiff fight against the French cavalry the Germans were recalled by the bugle and those that remained in the saddle struggled wearily back the way they had come, pursued by the French horse and shot at by the infantry. Less than half the brigade returned alive. Of the 310 Magdeburg Cuirassiers who had gone into action only 104 came out, while only 90 Uhlans answered the roll-call. But the sacrifice of two of Prussia's finest cavalry regiments had not been in vain. The French had received such a shock from the charge that, for the time being, they abandoned their attempt to encircle the German left and advance on Vionville and Flavigny.

113

The *Todtenritt* – 'Death Ride' – was the first in a series of cavalry versus cavalry actions that caused Mars-la-Tour to be described as the 'greatest cavalry battle of modern times'. In the final encounter of the day some 5,000 horsemen were engaged with sabre and lance. The long, sanguinary contest lasted 12 hours, leaving the blood-soaked ground littered with 32,000 dead, dying and wounded men and hundreds of dead and mutilated horses. It would appear to be a drawn battle, leaving the Germans with some advantage, and they went on to win the war. The *Todtenritt* entered German and cavalry history, never to be forgotten.

Late Victorian cartoon showing the rigours of a cavalry riding school.

The *Todtenritt* – 'Death Ride' – was the first in a series of cavalry versus cavalry actions that caused Mars-la-Tour to be described as the 'greatest cavalry battle of modern times'. In the final encounter of the day some 5,000 horsemen were engaged with sabre and lance. The long, sanguinary contest lasted 12 hours, leaving the blood-soaked ground littered with 32,000 dead, dying and wounded men and hundreds of dead and mutilated horses. It would appear to be a drawn battle, leaving the Germans with some advantage, and they went on to win the war. The *Todtenritt* entered German and cavalry history, never to be forgotten.

The last cavalry charge of note in the 19th century took place during the British campaign to reconquer the Sudan: the charge of the 21st Lancers at Omdurman on 2 September 1898. The Anglo-Egyptian army, commanded by General Kitchener, faced a formidable Dervish force ruled by the Khalifa Abdullahi, successor of the Madhi. The Dervish soldier was a fearless, fanatical warrior respected by his British foe. Kitchener moved up the Nile towards Khartoum, the capital of the Sudan. The enemy was encountered near Omdurman, a Dervish holy place for it contained the tomb of the

114

Charge of the 21st Lancers at
Omdurman, 2 September 1898.
Detail of the painting by E. Matthew
Hale.

revered Madhi. Early on 2 September the Dervish army attacked, but was repulsed by heavy artillery and infantry fire, Kitchener having deployed his force in a strong position on the bank of the Nile.

Immediately the enemy withdrew, Kitchener ordered the 21st Lancers to leave the lines and reconnoitre on the southern flank and if possible to prevent scattered groups of Dervishes from retiring to Omdurman, from which it would have been difficult to dislodge them. The 21st, 320 strong, was commanded by Lieutenant Colonel Martin. Riding with them was Lieutenant Winston Churchill of the 4th Hussars, on attachment to the 21st and commanding a troop. He was also acting as unofficial war correspondent for *The Morning Post.* The lancers wore khaki: jackets buttoned up to the neck, Bedford-cord pantaloons, sun helmets with khaki neck screens, and were armed with lance, sword and carbine. After eight years in India the regiment went to Egypt in 1896, the only British cavalry regiment in the force sent to reconquer the Sudan, and never having been in action before.

Trotting over the scrub-studded desert on their little Syrian horses the lancers came across a party of Dervishes, who opened fire. Colonel Martin decided to charge them. The trumpet sounded 'Right wheel into line', the 16 troops swung round and locked into a long galloping line, and the 21st Lancers were committed to their first charge in war. Colonel Martin, in the

The unglamorous side of being in the cavalry. British troopers 'mucking out' the horse stables in 1896.

lead, soon realised he had been led into a trap. The lancers were riding headlong towards a *khor* (dry river bed), hitherto unseen, that contained some 2,000 of the enemy who, having lain in wait concealed, were now on their feet eager to welcome the onrushing horsemen with bullets, spears and razor-sharp swords. The lancers plunged into a great maw of violence and death.

'The Dervishes showed no fear of cavalry,' wrote Churchill, 'and would not move unless you knocked them over with the horse. They tried to hamstring the horses, to cut the bridles and reins, and slashed and stabbed in all directions and fired rifles at a few feet range.'

Churchill had purchased in London a Mauser automatic pistol, Model 1896, with a ten-round box magazine. And this he chose to use in the charge, rather than his sword:

'We emerged into a region of scattered men and personal combats. The troop broke up and disappeared. I pulled up into a trot and rode up to individuals firing my pistol in their faces... Then I looked round and saw the Dervish mass reforming... I saw two men get down on their knees and take aim [at me] with rifles, and for the first time the danger and peril came home to me. I turned and galloped. The squadron was reforming nearly 150 yards away... I pulled into a canter and rejoined my troop – having fired exactly ten shots and emptied my pistol – but

116

Winston Churchill in the uniform of the 4th Hussars. During the battle of Omdurman he was attached to the 21st Lancers and commanded a troop in the famous charge.

without a hair of my horse or a stitch of my clothing being touched. Very few can say the same.'

Churchill was indeed fortunate to come through unscathed. Hardly a man or horse escaped without some injury, some slight, but in many cases serious. The centre squadron, striking the Dervish line where the crowd was thickest, suffered most. Riders who fell were virtually doomed as the enemy pounced upon them. Lieutenant the Honourable R.F. Molyneux, Royal Horse Guards, attached to the lancers, had his horse shot dead under him just before reaching the *khor*. He ran into the mêlée, revolver in hand. Two warriors attacked him. He shot one but the other slashed his arm,

117

Lieutenant-Colonel R. H. Martin leading the 21st Lancers against the Dervishes at Omdurman. Illustration by John Charlton. It was the last grand cavalry charge of the 19th century.

making him drop his gun. Surrounded by the enemy he called for help to a lancer passing by, Private Byrne, himself badly wounded by bullet and spear. Byrne, unable to use a weapon, barged the warriors aside with his horse and, although wounded again, managed to get Molyneux to safety. Byrne was one of three lancers to win the Victoria Cross that day.

Surgeon-Major Pinches, whose horse had been shot under him, was saved by Sergeant-Major Brennan who, after cutting down several of his assailants, got the major up behind him on horse and rode out of the *khor*. Lieutenant Grenfell, leading a troop of the centre squadron, was thrown from his wounded horse and made a desperate stand. Having emptied his revolver at the closing enemy, he was last seen alive fighting with his sword. When his watch was recovered by his brother after the fight it was found to have been pierced by a spear which stopped it at 8.40.

In about two minutes the 21st had suffered more than 70 casualties: one officer and 20 men dead, four officers and 46 men wounded, 119 horses killed or wounded. Having re-formed, the lancers were ready to charge back through the enemy, but Colonel Martin decided that enough had been done on horseback. He moved to a flank position, dismounted his men and opened deadly enfilade fire down the *khor* with carbines, compelling the Dervishes to vacate the dangerous place and scatter to the shelter of the hills.

Kitchener defeated the Dervish army and the 21st Lancers won fame for their gallant but costly charge. Queen Victoria honoured the regiment by bestowing the additional title of the 21st (Empress of India's) Lancers. In 1922 the regiment was merged with the 17th Lancers to form the 17th/21st Lancers, serving as an armoured regiment in the British Army of today.

4 · THE COSSACKS

For centuries the cossacks imposed their remarkable presence on the consciousness of the Russian people. These fierce riders of the steppes served as warrior-colonists in the wilderness regions of the tsar's immense empire. They were employed as frontier guardians to keep at bay the Tatar nomads and other predatory tribesmen. Cossacks fought as part of the Russian army in foreign wars. During moments of public protest and demonstration they were used by the tsarists as repressive gendarmerie and earned notoriety for their brutality in crowd control.

On campaign cossacks ranked high among the finest of light cavalry, probably unexcelled in scouting and vedette duties: 'The army may sleep safely when cossacks are at the outposts,' Frank D. Millet wrote in Harper's New Monthly Magazine, January 1887. In skirmishing and raiding they were bold yet prudent; in pursuit of a fleeing enemy they were implacable and without mercy. Their superb horsemanship, free spirit, and swaggering pride in their colourful identity and long martial tradition placed them apart from other Russians.

The original cossacks were the Tatar nomads who swept over Russia and central Europe with the Mongol-Tatar hordes of Ghengis Khan, and later his sons. When the great hordes broke up the Tatars formed small tribal groups and roamed the steppes, the vast treeless plains of south and south-east Russia, which became known as Tatary, raiding and robbing and stealing horses. The Russian principalities were forced to come to terms with these savage unconquerable horsemen and paid them homage and tribute. In the 15th century the Muscovites, the Poles and Lithuanians hired mercenary Tatar tribes to combat Tatar incursions and guard the frontiers. These were the first Russian cossacks. The name 'cossack' comes from the Tatar word *kazak* meaning 'free warrior' and today a part of old Tatary is known as Kazakhstan.

As more Slavonic settlers migrated southward in the 16th century they began to displace the Tatar cossacks, adopting and adapting the Tatar lifestyle. The Tatar rode with short stirrup leathers, jockey fashion; he did not wear spurs but urged on his mount with a short whip attached to his wrist. His weapons were a short bow from which he could shoot arrows accurately at the gallop, a lance, a curved sword, a small shield, and a heavy club. The Slav or Russian cossack communities grew in numbers and spread throughout the Ukraine and the Caucasus and mostly took their names from the rivers by which they settled: the Don, the Ural, Kuban and

A tatar-style cossack drawn from
life by the American artist Frederic
Remington in 1893. Note the crude
wooden lance.

Terek. There were also Astrakhan, Orenburg, and Siberian cossacks and
numerous other tribes and subtribes inhabiting parts of Russia, Poland,
Tatary and Turkey.

These early Russian cossacks were not subject to the rule of Muscovy,
the ancient principality of Moscow, which in the 16th and 17th centuries
included the whole of European Russia. Cossack communities elected their
own leader, known as the *hetman* or *ataman*. Cossacks were always at war
with each other, and they would attack Russian, Tatar, Turk, Pole and
Lithuanian alike for plunder and profit. They were brigands, raiding and
pillaging towns and settlements and merchant caravans. In 1571 the Don
cossacks and Moscow made a deal in which Moscow would pay them gold,

121

gunpow᠁ ᠁nd other goods to range the frontier steppes and guard against ᠁cursions by the Tatars and Circassians.

Stefan Batory, elected King of Poland in 1575, absorbed the Ukrainian cossacks as militiamen, exempting them from taxes and allowing them to hold land under privileged conditions. In return the cossacks supplied irregular regiments in time of war and guarded the frontier against other cossacks. Later, Batory imposed his own choice of *hetman* on the Ukrainians, usually a high-ranking army officer based in Warsaw. Eventually this happened to all Russian cossacks. The wild Russian horsemen were finally tamed and harnessed to the crown during the successive reigns of Peter the Great, Catherine the Great, and Nicholas I. There were, however, many revolts before the cossacks submitted. They held their land by military tenure and, although under firm control of Moscow, retained a large measure of independence, privilege and individuality from the rest of the army. The free warrior spirit still burned brightly and the cossack boasted that 'he did not remove his hat even before the Tsar'.

A cossack was born to the saddle and a warrior's life. The first sounds he heard were the words of martial songs by which he was rocked to sleep. Almost before they learned to walk the boys were placed on horseback. Cossacks were generally small in stature and slightly built, a result of intermarriage between Slav and Tatar. Their communities were moved and planted wherever central government saw fit to have soldier-colonists to hold and develop land and guard the borders of the ever-expanding Russian empire. These border outpost settlements (known as *stanitsa*)

122

formed what was called the military line, hence the term 'Cossacks of the Line'. All along the frontier, sentinels were posted in high lookout scaffolds. Every village had a cannon to be fired to warn the neighbouring *stanitsa* of the approach of danger.

When the tsar called for soldiers to fight a war the cossacks mobilised quickly, bringing their own horses, arms and other equipment. From his Tatar paradigm the Russian cossack retained the sabre and lance, and only the Asian cossacks held on to the short bow; Turkic-Bashkir archers served Russia in the Napoleonic war and against the Kirghiz Tatars in the 1820s. Later cossacks carried carbines in special skin or canvas cases slung on their backs. The sabre had no hilt or crossguard and was kept in a wood and leather scabbard. All cossack equipment, horse and man, was contrived to make the minimum amount of noise when on the move. Captain Nolan, the man who delivered the message that launched the Charge of the Light

The incident in which a daring cossack nearly captured and killed Napoleon, but was shot down at the last moment by the emperor's aide.

124

During the French retreat from Russia, Turkic-Bashkir cossack archers hounded and harried the demoralised once-grand army.

Brigade, declared that 'A hundred cossacks make less noise than a single regular cavalry soldier.'

The cossack remained a soldier for most of his active life. In 1835 Don cossacks, for example, were liable to serve 30 years in the service of the tsar, this term being divided between active service with the army and *stanitsa* duties. Service was later shortened and split into three periods: *stanitsa* service, foreign field service, and reserve, the latter requiring the veteran cossack to keep horse and equipment ready for war service.

The cossacks, especially those of the Don, who provided more regiments than all the other cossack communities, served Alexander I exceedingly well in the war of 1812 and became the scourge of Napoleon's Grand Army. Napoleon, much to his chagrin, discounted the cossacks, whom he called 'the disgrace of the human race'. For it was the cossacks who compounded the agony of the wicked Russian winter and greatly

125

contributed to the destruction of the once-grand army in the retreat from Moscow. They relentlessly pursued the fleeing French, hacking and harrying the ragged, dispirited invaders as they struggled over the hostile frozen land.

The Imperial Stud at Prevallie, reserved exclusively for cossack cavalry. Illustration of the 1880s.

Napoleon invaded Russian territory in June 1812. While he found the Russian army elusive and difficult to bring to battle, his soldiers ran into cossacks everywhere. The ubiquitous horsemen covered the Russian withdrawals, they kept the French movements under constant observation, they operated behind enemy lines, they raided supply trains, they burned houses and devastated the countryside to deny the invaders any sustenance. They plagued the French night and day, always appearing where least expected. When faced with an aggressive body of regular cavalry, the wolf-like cossacks melted away, sensibly, to strike another day.

So bold were the cossacks that on one occasion a patrol nearly succeeded in capturing and killing Napoleon himself. One cossack rode right up to the emperor but was shot down at the last minute by a staff officer. 'The Cossacks', in the opinion of the French General de Brack, 'were an arm which rendered the war highly dangerous, especially to such of our officers as we entrusted with making reconnaissance. Many among them, and especially of the general staff, preferred forwarding the reports which they received from the peasantry, rather than going a distance and exposing

126

A cossack of the Don. Illustration of the 1880s.

themselves to the attacks of the Cossacks. The Emperor, therefore, could no longer know the state of affairs.'

Another French general, Morand, made the following perceptive assessment of the cossacks from first-hand experience:

'These rude horsemen are ignorant of our divisions, of our regular alignements, of all that order which we so overweeningly estimate. Their custom is to keep their horses close between their legs; their feet rest in broad stirrups, which support them when they use their weapons. They spring from a state of rest to the full gallop, and at the gallop they make a dead halt. Their horses second their skill, and seem only part of themselves. These men are always on the alert, they move with extraordinary rapidity, have few wants, and are full of warlike ardour.'

A cossack of Astrakhan.

This war saw the cossacks, not yet fully Russianised and their savage spirit still undiluted, at their warrior best. Their natural scouting abilities, their hardiness, their martial cunning, were all at optimum condition. General Morand describes how the hitherto despised cossacks were able to outwit, outmanoeuvre and destroy piecemeal the finest of French regular cavalry supported by infantry and artillery.

'What a magnificent spectacle was that of the French cavalry flashing in gold and steel under the rays of a June sun, extending its lines upon the flanks of the hills of the Niemen, and burning with eagerness and courage! What bitter reflections are those of the ineffectual manoeuvres which exhausted it against the Cossacks, those irregular forces until then so despised, but which did more for Russia than all the regular armies of that empire! Every day they were to be seen on the horizon, extending over an immense line, whilst their daring flankers came and braved us even in our ranks. We formed and marched against the line, which, the moment we reached it, vanished, and the horizon no longer showed anything but birch trees and pines. But an hour afterwards, whilst our horses were feeding, the attack was

A trumpeter of the Kuban cossack regiment, Imperial Guard Corps, drawn from life by the American artist Frederic Remington in 1893.

A cossack of the line, a type who manned the border settlements that formed the military line. He wears the customary *kinzhal* or dagger and carries his carbine, slung over his back, in a shaggy animal-skin case.

resumed and a black line again presented itself; the same manoeuvres were resumed, which were followed by the same result.'

Thus it was that the finest and bravest of European cavalry exhausted and wasted itself against irregular horsemen deemed unworthy of French valour and arms, but 'who nevertheless,' in the words of Morand, 'were sufficient to save the empire, of which they are the real support and sole deliverers... The Cossacks returned covered with spoils and glory to the fertile banks of the Danaetz [Donets], whilst the soil of Russia was strewn with the carcases and arms of our warriors.'

Like its rider, the cossack horse was at its primitive best in the Napoleonic period. The steppe pony was small and sturdy; a tough, wiry beast, short of limb and neck and possessed of remarkable stamina. Indifferent to weather, it thrived on poor food; even in the depths of winter it could survive on the little grass its unshod feet could scrape from under the snow, and still carry its rider 50 miles a day. Ugly to Western eyes, the

129

cossack mount appeared 'mean in shape and slouching in motion,' according to Sir Robert Ker Porter, 'every limb speaks of languor and every moment you expect to see them drop dead under their heavy burthen – but so false are these shows that there is not a more hardy animal existing.' Major-General Sir Robert Wilson noted that Don cossacks were 'mounted on a very little, ill-conditioned horse that could walk at the rate of five miles an hour with ease, or dispute the race with the swiftest.'

The cossack rode Tatar style without spurs and carried a short whip, called the *nagaika*, attached to his wrist. He did not treat his mount cruelly, neither did he kill it with kindness, but most cossacks of the old type had an amazing affinity with their horses, and the animal would very often obey no other rider. Without equal in scouting, vedette duties and skirmishing the cossacks rarely mounted a mass charge in the formalised style traditional to Western European cavalry. Cossacks were essentially

130

'Cossack Drill – Rescuing the Wounded', by Remington. The cossacks perfected this method of picking up an injured comrade on the field of battle.

light horsemen, the eyes and ears of the army, and not particularly suited to the knee to knee shock charge.

However, when they did attack *en masse* they did so in extended order that developed into a crescent formation, called the *lava*: this was long enough to envelop the enemy's flanks, threaten his rear, and fragment the opposing force into single combat. A form of attack adopted from the Tatar cossacks, Russian cavalry regulations of 1884 stated that the *lava* 'is used not only in the attack but also for purposes of manoeuvre, and particularly in cases where it is desirable to avoid conflict with a solid body of the enemy, but at the same time desirable to constantly harass him or to wear him out upon his front and flanks, or to coax him to attack in open order, or to engage him in single combat, in which the latter particularly the Cossacks, by means of their skilful management when alone, are expected to be superior to regular cavalry accustomed to move in solid bodies.'

Although most cossacks were consummate horsemen, only a relatively few were masters of the spectacular trick riding called *dzhigitovka*, originally performed by the Circassians. Regiments had special sections that trained and exercised in equestrian gymnastics for military displays. Western observers were always impressed by the cossack exhibition of *dzhigitovka*. 'They perform feats which would turn a cowboy green with envy,' commented an American officer, 'such tricks as I have never seen in any circus. The men swinging from the pommel of their saddles while at the full gallop; springing from one side of their horses to the other side, and turning somersaults.' Then, as a grand finale, the champion rider 'performed all these dangerous tricks with a sabre clenched between his

teeth'. The Circassians were generally regarded as the boldest and most skilful of cossack riders. Captain Nolan wrote about them in his book published in 1853.

'The Circassians are unsurpassed in the management of their war-horses and arms, and so proud of their skill that, whereas most [soldiers of other] nations show wounds received in action as honourable scars, the Circassians hide them as silent witnesses of their awkwardness and want of address in single combat. At the Russian reviews in 1852 I saw a few sheets of paper placed on the ground opposite the Emperor: he gave a signal to some Circassians formed in line a few hundred yards off. Down they all came at speed racing with one another. The first up fired at the marks either with pistol or carbine; the sheets of paper flew up in pieces: those who followed fired into the fragments that were at hand, blowing them to atoms.'

Like other cossack people the Circassians were for many years engaged in rebellions and wars against Russian domination. Many Circassians fled to Turkey and joined the army. During the Russo-Turkish war of 1877-78 a Don cossack force of three squadrons went on a foraging and reconnoitring

133

Cossacks of the Imperial Guard in 1900.

expedition in the direction of the Black Sea. The Dons encountered a force of Turkish Circassians of similar strength. 'My men,' said the major in command of the Dons, 'were eager for a fight without delay, but I thought a little caution was necessary, so I deployed them in line just behind the hill and waited.' A few minutes later a Circassian officer appeared on the other side riding out from his column, which he had halted at the sight of the enemy. He pranced about on a splendid black horse, making all kinds of

A fierce cavalry encounter during the Russo-Japanese War. Painting by G. Hoseda.

defiant and insulting gestures that every cossack knew to mean a challenge to single combat.

'Of course,' said the Don cossack major, 'the only proper thing for me to do was to disregard all such insults and challenges and leave the medieval mode of warfare to Circassians and savages. But there was something in the air, I can't explain what. I could see my men watching me eagerly to see what I would do. I thought of the stories my father used to tell – how he fought the Turcomans in single combat. I glanced at the dagger hanging at my belt, a relic of one of those fights. The next thing I was conscious of I was laying my *nagaika* across the flanks of my horse and we were flying down the grassy slope. There I met the Circassian and after a few strokes with my sabre he fell from his horse. My men galloped up with a cheer, routed the enemy and captured their camp, some distance farther on, with the dinner cooking in the pots.'

The Don cossacks returned to camp laden with spoils, behind the major at the head of the column, an orderly led the Circassian's black horse with richly ornamented bridle and saddle. The major carried his dead antagonist's silver mounted sword, dagger and pistol.

For many years plunder was the natural concomitant of war for the cossacks. During that time a succession of foreign wars gave the cossacks so much opportunity for loot that they represented a very prosperous section

135

of the Russian people. The American Frank Millet rode with the Russian
cossacks in the Russo-Turkish War of 1877-78 and he observed 'all sorts of
promiscuous plunder being brought into camp, making the Circassian
quarters look more like a robber's den than a military shelter.' Millet, a
journalist-illustrator, penned an interesting account of his experiences
with the cossacks. Here he describes the dress and weapons of the
Circassians:

'They wear at all seasons of the year a high cylindrical hat of Astrakhan wool,
usually black with a top of cloth or velvet. The coat is similar in pattern to the
Russian Cossack coat [the *cherkesska*], but the skirts are usually longer and fuller and
the sleeves broad at the bottom. The outside coat has no collar but is cut low in
front to disclose a red undercoat hooked high in the neck. Full trousers and boots
complete the ordinary dress. In place of the grey Russian overcoat they carry a
bourka [or *burka*], a circular cloak that is waterproof and windproof and ample
enough when worn on horseback to cover the rider completely and part of his
horse as well. It serves also as a bed by night. Circassian arms are quite as

characterisic as their dress. A Berdan carbine [an American weapon manufactured under licence] is slung across the back in a case of shaggy goat-skin. The sabre is a guardless one, like those carried by Russian cossacks, and is hung from the shoulder by a narrow strap. From the waist belt dangles in front a long, pointed dagger [the *kinzhal*], and behind, a quaint flintlock pistol altered to the percussion system, and with a large round knob on the butt. One of the most curious portions of Circassian dress is the row of cylindrical cases which fit into cloth pockets on the breast of the coat, ten either side. In the days of muzzle-loading guns these held a cartridge apiece, and a tiny flask of priming powder hung around the neck. The cases are still preserved as a portion of the regulation dress, chiefly as ornament, partly to hold charges for the pistol, which still remains of the antique pattern, but largely for the more prosaic purpose of holding salt, tea, and various trifles... At all times, but particularly in winter, when the *bourka* and the *bashlik* [pointed hood] were worn, the Circassian Cossacks presented a decidedly savage and warlike appearance.'

By the 1880s cossack military dress had become standardised on the Russian army pattern: field service tunic blouse with shoulder straps in the regimental colour, peaked or peakless service cap, baggy blue-grey trousers

137

with stripe the same colour as shoulder straps, high boots, and grey-brown greatcoat. Only the Kuban and Terek cossack regiments (largely composed of Circassians) retained the traditional Circassian style *cherkesska*, fur hat, and *bourka* cloak. The nominal strength of a cossack regiment in peacetime was 1,000 men, consisting of six *sotnias* or squadrons. A cavalry division of the Russian army was composed of four regiments: one of dragoons, one of lancers, one of hussars and one of cossacks. According to the official statement of 1892 the six cossack armies or communities of European Russia were expected in wartime to furnish the following fighting force, composed of cavalry, horse artillery and infantry, of roughly 150,000 men:

Cossack Army			
officers and men			
Don	64,069	Terek	11,519
Kuban	44,806	Ural	8,352
Orenburg	18,866	Astrakhan	1,950

Cossacks destroying telegraph lines in the Russo-Japanese war.

With the coming of the 20th century the cossack (now thoroughly Russianised: his privileges and his traditional military character undermined by governmental interference, his people diluted by growing numbers of peasants imposed upon him for administrative reasons) was but a shadow of his former self. During the Russian grand manoeuvres of 1891 General Gurko voiced the critical opinion that any attempt of the cossacks to fire from the saddle should be stopped because the modern cossack had lost so much of his skill with the rifle that he was no better marksman on horseback than any trooper in the other cavalry regiments.

Cossacks charging Austrian infantry and artillery in the Carpathians during World War 1, as imagined by an illustrator.

On the eve of the Russo-Japanese War of 1904-05 General Fujii, Commandant of the Staff College, had this to say in his study of the Russian army:

'Russian cavalry and sometimes infantry when retreating set fire to villages, so that we cannot expect to find shelter and supplies in the places they have evacuated. The Cossacks often attack transport trains and lines of communication, and it is always necessary to keep close watch on both flanks. If once successful in these attacks they will make many attempts. The Cossack in the war of 1877 [against the Turks] made no heroic movement. His reputation is built entirely on his own reports, which are always exaggerated. He invariably retires when met by a stronger force. If our infantry is prepared we need have no fear of the Cossack.'

A Russian study of the Japanese army of 1904 considered the cavalry horses very poor, weak, and badly trained, that every trooper rode after his own fashion and, generally, his seat was neither well-balanced nor easy. The report continues that the Japanese used curb and snaffle all the time, that the speed of the horses was not well regulated, the horses did not trot and the cavalry did not keep together. The study claimed that these defects showed that the Japanese lacked good cavalry instructors and were not trained in the management of horses. Further criticism stated that

141

A cossack in exile giving a display of trick riding in England in the 1930s.

Japanese cavalry equipment was not uniformly and scientifically made; the saddle often being on the withers of the horses so that when they moved quickly the riders were much shaken, and the animals developed saddle galls and fistulous withers.

In refuting a number of these statements a Japanese cavalry officer answered that a Japanese cavalry trooper could 'march 25 miles a day, and on a good road can trot seven-and-a-half miles an hour – a little quicker than the Russian horses and a trifle slower than the German. Judging by camps, the speed of the Russian cavalry is not greater than our cavalry.' The Russian study also noted that 'The duties of [Japanese] reconnaissance and cavalry patrols are the same as in the Russian army. Their reports are usually very detailed, accurate, and trustworthy. When a cavalry patrol meets an enemy it takes up a defensive position.' Japanese cavalrymen were well trained in the use of the carbine and were skilful swordsmen, their blades being very sharp. They had little use for the lance.

During the Russo-Japanese war the cossacks performed their usual duties of reconnaissance, patrol, picket and guard. They also mounted raids on enemy supply bases, cut railway lines and destroyed telegraph posts. There were a number of cavalry encounters but nothing of significance. The inferiority of the Japanese cavalry was atoned for to some extent by the extreme mobility of the infantry who could, it was claimed, march 20 miles day after day, and on occasion 40 miles in a day. In a fierce cavalry

Prince Kanin leading his Japanese cavalry brigade against the Russians in the battle of Sha-ho. Painted by Suko.

engagment at Pu-lang-tien, Lance-corporal Saijiro Toriyama received a serious head wound and a cut above his right ear, and was pierced through the neck to his tongue. He recovered from his dreadful injuries and recorded his battle experience:

'During the afternoon of 29th May 1904 as we advanced toward Pu-lang-tien we saw the Russians in the distance and next day we fell in with them at about 1 p.m. We dashed so near to them that soon a hand-to-hand combat commenced. In five minutes or so another body of Russian cavalry carrying a regimental flag made their appearance suddenly on our flank and we found ourselves completely surrounded by the enemy who evidently outnumbered us five or six fold. We now made up our minds to die on the spot after killing as many Russians as we could, and dashed fiercely at the enemy. We fought with swords and they with spears and swords. The Russians in front gave way and those behind pressed on me. I fought with my back against that of my comrade. While thus fighting, my comrade's horse gave a sudden jump which startled my horse and in another moment I cut down a Russian. Then I saw our chief officer fighting furiously, surrounded by Cossacks. I galloped to his rescue and dealt several desperate blows with my sword here and there at

143

Cossacks who served under the Nazi banner during World War 2.

some Russians whose spears pierced at me with no great effect. Finally, exhausted with fatigue, my nerves strained, my eyes became dim so that I could no more distinguish friend from foe. I thought of committing *harakiri*, but before doing that I wished to kill one more Russian. I continued to fight till my horse was hit and I fell prostrate on the ground unconscious. The bursting of a shell revived me, and, finding my sword still in my hand, I got up. I saw a Cossack awaking in the same manner at the same sound. I kicked him and cut him down before he thrust his lance at me. The scene was witnessed by about 20 Cossacks 100 yards away, who quickly attacked me. For a few minutes I fought but soon I fell with a cold chill

144

Cossacks of the Red Army in World War 2. Warfare had changed greatly and so had the cossack, a pale shadow of the former rider of the steppes.

down my back and neck, and knew nothing further. In this unconscious state I lay till I was picked up by our medical men.'

In World War I the cossack regiments were inefficiently commanded and misused. A number of units designated 'Cossack' were not cossack at all. Some cossack horse regiments were employed as line infantry and suffered heavy casualties. Other regiments were fragmented and used as escorts for POWs, as despatch riders, to round up Russian stragglers and deserters, and to prevent reluctant soldiers from defecting from the front line. For propaganda purposes central government circulated fictitious accounts of the 'dreaded cossacks' routing enemy forces in gallant 'death or glory' charges, and highly imaginative war illustrators had a field day depicting galloping cossacks in spectacular action against the Austrians and Germans.

As the war went from bad to worse for the Russian army, the nation's living conditions and public morale deteriorated. The war-weary Russian people responded with strikes, demonstrations and revolution. In the late 19th century and the early years of the 20th century the cossacks were used in the name of the tsar to put down internal discontent and protest

which threatened his autocratic power. The cossacks dispersed the crowds with brutal use of the sword, the whip, and trampling hooves. They became the hated symbol of tsarist oppression and the term 'cossack' became synonymous throughout the world with ruthless gendarme activity. In February 1917, however, when the capital Petrograd was in a state of revolution, Don cossack regiments and the Kuban Terek royal guard refused to move against soldier mutineers and indeed joined them in their cause. This cossack defection hastened the abdication of the tsar.

In the savage civil war that followed the cossacks were divided in their loyalty: some fought for the Red Army, others supported the opposing White or tsarist forces. When the communists came to power after the civil war, central government viewed all cossacks as hostile to the new regime and set about to destroy what was left of their privileges, their culture, and their special character, in order to submerge the cossack people into the

146

uniform mass of the new Soviet state. The Red Army destroyed cossack villages and settlements and killed or deported the inhabitants. The wearing of traditional cossack dress and the singing of cossack songs were prohibited on pain of death.

Many cossacks fled the country and lived abroad, some giving displays of trick riding or becoming riding masters. Others stayed in Russia and fought back, becoming outlaws and brigands, reverting to their role of centuries before. In the Kuban, cossacks repelled the Red cavalry sent against them and held out for years. One of the most celebrated of Kuban cossack rebels was Dunko, who escaped from prison and sought the sanctuary of the steppe. He became leader of a small band and carried out raids against government forces. He was eventually surrounded and chose to die in battle rather than surrender.

Having snuffed out the flame of Cossackdom, the Soviet state then saw fit – when the Germans invaded Russia in 1941 – to rekindle it in the national interest. Several Red Army cavalry divisions were designated 'Cossack' and horse soldiers were recruited in the Caucasus and other cossack regions to serve in newly raised cossack formations. Only a small number of these recruits were true cossacks. The Soviet style cossack was armed with carbine and sword but no lance; he did not carry the traditional wrist-whip and he wore spurs. Why this wide use of cavalry in modern warfare? 'If we had more trucks and tanks,' General Malinovsky explained, 'we would have used less cavalry.'

The Soviet government, like the tsarist one, disseminated propaganda stories abroad of heroic exploits carried out by the 'cossack sons of the Soviet Union'. Although many of these stories were fabricated or highly exaggerated, General Lev Dovator did win fame by leading Don cossacks on missions behind German lines. During one operation they covered a frozen river near Rostov with their *bourkas* to muffle the hoof beats. It was claimed that at the end of 1941 cossacks operating with Rokossovsky's army west of Moscow made a sabre charge on a German motorised column one moonlit night and captured 300 vehicles, 100 pieces of artillery and other weapons.

The German invaders sought to exploit the anti-Soviet cossack elements and raised auxiliary cossack formations from POWs and willing recruits in occupied lands to fight against the Red Army. These units were of negative military value. After the war the surviving cossack peoples were absorbed into the general life of the Soviet Union. The proud cossack of old Russia had gone forever, only his hoof-beats in history remain.

5 · SOWARS AND SUN HELMETS

For more than a century Indian cavalry regiments served the British Crown with great distinction in minor and major wars and numerous small campaigns. The British officers who commanded the turbanned *sowars* (troopers) were extremely proud of their warrior horsemen, who in dash and discipline equalled their British counterparts. For their part the Indian cavalrymen had high regard for their white sahibs and loyally served Queen Victoria and her successors until the British granted India independence in 1947. In the old days of the Raj it was the custom on certain occasions for the native officers of a regiment to visit their white officers and tender their respects.

'As each of the stalwart, bearded, soldierly-looking group entered the verandah,' wrote an eyewitness, 'he offered the hilt of his sword to his host in courteous signification of the fact that it and its owner were at his service. Not an atom of servility was noticeable, but rather a marked manliness and courtesy in bearing and conversation that stamped each man in the group as unmistakably a soldier and a gentleman.'

Recruited from the martial races − such as the Sikhs, Dogras, Pathans, Punjabis, Jats and Rajputs − Indian cavalry regiments were as brave in battle as they were resplendent on parade. Sir Charles Dilke, in 1881, described the 18th Bengal Lancers as 'beyond all question the finest looking cavalry regiment that I have ever seen.' Lieutenant-General Sir Robert Baden-Powell regarded the Indian cavalry as 'soldiers by birth and upbringing, and splendid horsemen and swordsmen.' Lord Roberts, who served for many years in India, made the following comment on a tour of inspection in 1889.

'The gallant Rajput horsemen of the Jhodpur Lancers had always been famous for their chivalrous bravery, unswerving fidelity and fearless self-devotion in their wars with the Mahrattas and the armies of the Mogul emperors, and I felt, as the superbly mounted squadrons passed before me, that they had lost none of their characteristics, and that blood and breeding must tell, and would, if put to the test, achieve the same results now as of old.'

Until the reorganisation of the Indian Army in 1861, following the great upheaval of the Indian Mutiny of 1857-58, British forces and native soldiers (sepoys) were under the control of the Honourable East India Company, a powerful institution originally created under royal charter for

Types of the 18th Bengal Lancers in the 1890s.

purely commercial purposes that entered upon a career of territorial acquisition. The red-coated armies of the East India Company, notably under Robert Clive, a former clerk in the Company's employment, secured a number of victories over the French and various Indian rulers and established British supremacy in India. After the Mutiny all powers of the Company were vested in the British Crown and the Indian troops became 'Soldiers of the Queen' and, it seems, were proud and privileged to be so.

With French military power broken in India, French soldiers of fortune offered their services to native rulers who were opposed to the East India Company and trained their soldiers on the European model. At the beginning of the 19th century the Mahratta Confederacy had reached its zenith in India and the ambitions of British policy brought the two powers into conflict. The Mahrattas, a Hindu martial race, were masters over territorial or tributary possessions some five times greater than those of the British. Five powerful chiefs – Peshwa, Holkar, Scindia, Bhonsla, and Gaekwar – dominated the Confederacy. Each of these warlords maintained an immense feudal army of predatory horsemen. A Frenchman named de

149

Boigne entered the service of Scindia and drilled his wild horsemen and foot soldiers in the European style. De Boigne and his Mahratta brigades won many battles in central and western India.

William Gardner, an ex-British officer, entered the service of Holkar and trained and commanded some troops. When the Mahratta chief accused him of treachery, Gardner attempted to kill him and escaped on a horse. He then offered his sword to Peshwa but when the Mahrattas went to war with the British, Gardner chose to fight with his countrymen. He was given command of a regiment of Jaipur irregulars and saw action against Holkar. Later, in 1809, he was ordered to raise a regiment of native irregulars that became famous as Gardner's Horse, a splendid body of cavalry dressed in red turban, long green coat adorned with silver lace, and red pyjamas, or loose trousers. Gardner's Horse became, in 1890, the 2nd Bengal Lancers.

The 2nd Bombay Lancers in review order of the 1880s. Painted by Richard Simkin.

Chief of the 'Jekranee Beloochees'. Scene in the Bolan Pass during the campaign of 1839.

Ressaldar (troop commander) Gurdath Singh, 12th Bengal Cavalry, and his orderly. Splendid examples of Sikh soldiers.

James Skinner was another celebrated leader of native irregular cavalry. Born of a Rajput girl and a Scots officer in the service of the East India Company, the half-caste Skinner was debarred from service with the Company because of his mixed parentage. An adventurous soul with military aspirations, he joined Scindia's army and served with distinction under de Boigne. He left the Mahratta army in 1803 and joined the British, raising and leading a regiment that became famous as Skinner's Horse, nicknamed 'The Yellow Boys' from their canary yellow coats. Skinner's Horse served the British well in the Second Mahratta War of 1803–05.

Irregular native cavalry regiments functioned on the *silladar* principle. Each man provided his own horse, accoutrements, clothing, weapons, and suchlike in return for a higher rate of pay than the regular or non-*silladar* cavalryman, for whom the government provided everything. The government provided ammunition, and in some cases firearms, and medical stores free to *silladar* regiments. To ensure uniformity an irregular regiment would provide a recruit with a horse and the required equipment, for which the recruit would pay back. Because of their tradition of self-maintenance (the system, considerably developed, prevailed in the Indian Army into the 20th century) *silladar* regiments nurtured an intense *esprit de corps*.

Mahratta horsemen of the early 19th century.

153

The Third Light Dragoons charge the Sikh guns at Aliwal in January 1846 during the First Sikh War. Painted by Stanley L. Wood.

The Second Mahratta War brought Sir Arthur Wellesley (later the Duke of Wellington) to prominence. In the battle of Assaye, 23 September 1803, Wellesley found himself facing a combined Mahratta army far outnumbering his own. He commanded a total of 4,500 men, of whom 1,170 (the 74th and 78th Regiments) were British infantry, 2,000 sepoys, 1,200 cavalry and 150 guns. The enemy had 17,000 foot soldiers, 115 guns and some 30,000 cavalry. No wonder 'the Mahrattas, numerous and daring as they were, stood astounded and appalled at the audacious spirit of this comparatively insignificant array that presumed to attack their formidable host'. It was indeed a prodigiously bold bid for fame and fortune and laid Wellesley open to a charge of rashness. 'But had I not attacked them,' he said in reply 'I would have been surrounded by their superior cavalry, my

Charge of the 14th King's Light Dragoons at Ramnuggar in November 1848, Second Sikh War. Detail of painting by H. Martens.

155

troops have starved, and I had nothing left but to hang myself to my tent pole!'

The battle reached a critical stage when the 74th Regiment was pounded into ruin by the enemy artillery and trampled over by Mahratta horse. Wellesley ordered forward his cavalry. The 19th Light Dragoons drew 350 sabres and charged, followed by a regiment of native cavalry. They crashed into the enemy horse and drove them into the Juah River, pursued them to the other side, then recrossed and joined the British main line. Finally, after three hours of fighting, the Mahrattas began to waver. Their chiefs Scindia and the Rajah of Berar deserted them, and the Mahrattas broke and fled. One of their captains called the dragoons 'perfect war tigers' — 'large, powerful men, the weight of whose sabres almost annihilated us, whilst they unhorsed numbers of my troopers by merely riding against them'.

The Mahratta Wars lasted from 1778 to 1818 when the British gained supremacy in central India. If the Mahrattas had proved a formidable foe, the Sikhs of the Punjab were even more martial and difficult to overcome. It is incorrect to speak of the Sikhs as a race. In the proper sense they are a numerous religious sect embracing many of the Hindu tribes and races of the Punjab. The generic term 'Sikh' means disciple, and every Sikh adds Singh, meaning lion or warrior to his name. Early in the 19th century the

156

General Nicholson's Irregular Cavalry attack rebel sepoys during the Indian Mutiny. A contemporary engraving.

Sikh clans were welded together into a warlike nation by the remarkable Ranjit Singh, the 'Lion of Lahore'. He hired a number of French soldiers-of-fortune to train his army, especially in the use of artillery, in the disciplined European manner.

When Ranjit Singh died in 1839 the Punjab fell into a state of hostile anarchy with various leaders vying for power. Confident that it could defeat any enemy, the Sikh army crossed the Sutlej River in December 1845 to rampage in British territory. Sir Hugh Gough hastily gathered together a force of 12,000 men and marched to check the Sikh army. Gough's Bengal sepoys were in a poor state of discipline and were mortally afraid of the fierce Sikhs. The armies clashed on 18 December at Mudki, a 'sharp and sanguinary' battle in which the Sikhs were repulsed. On receiving reinforcements Gough followed up with an assault on the Sikhs at Ferozeshah, which forced them to retire across the Sutlej.

In January 1846 the Sikhs again crossed the river and met the British at Aliwal, a battle in which the combined powers of infantry, artillery and cavalry were successively and triumphantly brought into action by the British, commanded by Sir Harry Smith. In this fight the 16th (The Queen's) Lancers especially distinguished themselves. The regiment – nicknamed the 'Scarlet Lancers' from the colour of their jacket, the only lancer regiment to wear that colour in the British Army – had been 24

157

years in India, serving in a number of campaigns, being the first British regiment to use the lance in action, at the capture of Bhurtpore.

The battle opened with a smart cannonade from the Sikh guns, under which the British infantry deployed into line. The village of Aliwal was the key of the enemy's position and this was bravely stormed and taken. As Smith's foot regiments advanced, Major Lawrenson galloped his light battery of horse artillery to within a short distance of the Sikh guns, halted, wheeled round, and unlimbered with admirable speed and opened such a brisk and accurate fire that he forced many of the enemy gunners to quit their pieces. Smith now pressed the left and centre of the Sikh line. The cavalry delivered several daring and effective charges against guns and infantry, the latter forming into a triangle instead of the usual square. When the lancers broke through the head of this novel defence they were confronted by the base, bristling with bayonets. As the impetus of the charge carried the horsemen through the dense mass of steel and fire, the Sikhs flung themselves flat on the ground, seeking to escape the flying lances, then sprang up when the horsemen had passed, firing into their backs. The charge made by Captain Bere's squadron set the pattern for the following charges that day. Corporal Cowtan was there.

'When my squadron was ordered to charge,' Cowtan wrote, 'we cheered and moved on like a flash of lightning, clearing all before us – guns, cavalry, infantry. At the first charge I dismounted two cavalrymen. On retiring we passed through a

The 9th Lancers in action against the Sikhs at Chillianwallah in January 1849, as depicted by Stanley L. Wood.

158

square of infantry and I left three men on the ground killed or wounded. One fellow was taking deliberate aim at me when I put my horse at him, and just in time, for his priming [powder] blackened my face. Sergeant Brown was riding next to me and cleaving everyone down with his sword when his horse was shot under him, and before he reached the ground he received no less than a dozen sword cuts which killed him... Our lances seemed to paralyse them altogether and you may be sure we did not give them time to recover themselves.'

Elsewhere on the field two squadrons of the Scarlet Lancers under the regiment's acting commanding officer Major Rowland Smyth, were ordered by Smith to charge and take a battery of enemy guns recently brought into action. 'Now, 16th,' Smyth shouted to his men, 'I'm going to give the order to charge. Three cheers for the Queen!' Sergeant Gould, one of those who cheered loudly and rode in the charge, describes it:

Sir Harry Burnett Lumsden founded the Corps of Guides in 1846 and was its first commander.

'At a trumpet note to trot, off we moved. Down we swept on the guns. Very soon they were in our possession. A more exciting job followed – we had to charge a square of infantry [formed up behind the battery]. At them we went, bullets flying like hailstorm. Right in front of us a big sergeant, Harry Newsome, mounted on a grey, shouted "Hullo, boys, here goes for death or a commission!" and forced his charger over the front rank of kneeling Sikhs, bristling with bayonets. He leant over and grasped one of their standards, but fell from his horse pierced by 19 bayonet wounds. Into the gap made by Newsome we dashed, but they made fearful havoc among us. When we got out the other side of the square our troop had lost both lieutenants, the cornet, troop sergeant-major, and two sergeants. I was the only sergeant left... Back we went through the disorganised square, the Sikhs peppering us in all directions. One of the men had both arms frightfully slashed by a Sikh, who was down under his horse's feet and who made an upward cut at him. We retired to our own line. As we passed the general [Sir Harry Smith] he shouted "Well done 16th. You have covered yourselves with glory!" '

The British won the day but at a high cost in casualties. The 16th Lancers, chiefly instrumental in bringing victory, suffered 8 officers and more than 100 troopers killed or wounded. 'The Sikhs are worthy of our arms,' wrote lancer Captain Pearson. 'Even our Peninsular heroes [veterans] say they never saw more severe fighting.' The mutilated body of Lance-Corporal Mowbray, the regiment's finest lancer and *sabreur* was found with both lance and sword broken, within a circle of dead Sikhs. A trooper in Captain Bere's squadron describes what befell him personally in the fight. 'I delivered a [lance] point at one fellow, but could not reach him and was about to settle a second fellow when a blow from a sabre from behind severed my arm just above the wrist, and my hand, grasping the lance, fell to the ground.' He lived to tell the tale, having his arm amputated just below the elbow. One of those killed was young Cornet George Bigoe Williams. Captain Bere wrote to T. Bigoe Williams as follows:

Types of the Queen's Own Corps of Guides in 1897. The first soldiers, it is claimed, to wear khaki uniforms.

'Your late brother was attached to my squadron. After we had been standing under a heavy cannonade for about two hours, I was ordered with my squadron to go to the left with a native squadron and to watch and prevent the enemy turning our

160

flank. After having watched them for about an hour, the enemy cavalry charged the native squadron, on the extreme left, and drove them back upon my squadron... So I had nothing to do but charge them, and the native squadron then formed upon me. The enemy cavalry halted when they saw us coming... and we sent them flying in all directions... After I had gone through the enemy I was brought up by a fortified village, when my men rallied and were all well up together. To return to our position we had to charge a square of infantry which had formed up to oppose our return. It was in this charge (which we succeeded in riding through) that your poor brother fell, with 21 men, out of about 120. I suppose the square was 1,000 to 1,200 strong, so that any poor fellow who fell must have been cut to pieces in a moment, nothing could save them.'

General Sir Samuel James Browne served in the Corps of Guides. He lost his left arm winning the VC in the Indian Mutiny. In order to cope with his equipment he designed a special sword-belt and pistol holster – the 'Sam Browne belt'.

The First Sikh War was terminated by another triumph of British arms at Sobraon, in which the 16th again took a prominent part. Gough occupied Lahore and the Punjab became a British protectorate, one of the terms being the surrender of the great Koh-I-Noor diamond to Queen Victoria. The Scarlet Lancers sailed for England in August 1846 and were received as national heroes. The Sikhs sought revenge in a second war that began in April 1848. If Aliwal had been a 'brilliant battle' and decisive victory won in the teeth of bitter opposition, the battle of Chillianwallah, 13 January 1849, was a 'muddled' and indecisive affair for the British. Chillianwallah was preceded by a disastrous cavalry engagement at Ramnuggar, 22

The Corps of Guides in the 1880s. The Guides comprised both cavalry and infantry. Painted by Richard Simkin.

November 1848; a fight triggered by the horse artillery having to abandon a gun in the sandy stretch of a ford.

Sikh cavalry, under cover of their own artillery, crossed the stream in order to take the gun. William Havelock, colonel of the 14th Light Dragoons, asked permission of Lord Gough to attack the Sikh horsemen and save the gun. Gough consented and the 14th swept forward supported by the 4th Irregular Cavalry (later retitled 3rd Bengal Cavalry). In a few violent moments the Sikh horse were broken and scattered. Had Havelock halted, rallied his men and returned to his lines all would have been well. But the approach of another body of cavalry tempted him to destruction. Calling his men to follow him, Havelock dashed through the heavy sands, deeper yet into the mud and water where horses floundered and men were stuck helpless under Sikh grapeshot, musket fire, and the slashing tulwars (sabres) of the enemy light horsemen. The British lost 90 men and 140 horses killed or wounded. Havelock was mortally injured in close combat. Another prominent casualty was General Charles Cureton, adjutant-general of the army, who was killed while riding forward in an attempt to stop Havelock's ill-judged second charge. At Chillianwallah the Sikh horse made a number of successful charges against British and sepoy infantry and

captured several colours. The cavalry brigade on the right of the line came to grief. A 19th century account describes what happened:

'The brigade's four line regiments – led by an effete colonel who could scarcely mount his horse, got entangled in the brushwood and masked their own guns. While halted to restore cohesion, the old brigadier was wounded by a Sikh trooper: suddenly some caitiff gave the command "Three's about!" – from whose lips came the dastard cry was never ascertained. As the line went about, the pace quickened into a panic gallop, the British troopers followed closely by a few hundred derisive Sikh horsemen. Crowded together in their headlong flight, the fugitive dragoons [14th Light Dragoons] rode right through and over Christie's and Huish's batteries, disabling gunners, upsetting tumbrils, and carrying ruin and dismay far into the rear among the wounded and medical staff. Four guns fell into enemy hands... and not till Lane's gunners had poured some rounds of grapeshot into the pursuers, while a wing of the 9th Lancers once more confronted the enemy, were the Sikh horsemen daunted into a leisurely retreat.'

In spite of the foregoing debacle Chillianwallah can be claimed a technical British victory in that the enemy were compelled to quit the field. Gough however had little to show for 2,300 killed and wounded. He stood fast

163

until reinforcements reached him from Multan and then attacked the Sikhs at Gujerat, 21 February 1849, defeating them utterly and finally. The Sikhs fought with their usual fervour and stubbornness. Their cavalry hovered on either flank, eager to pass round into the British rear. A body of Sikh horse with a brigade of Afghan cavalry attempted an advance on Sir Joseph Thackwell's [the left] flank. He launched against them the Scinde Irregular Horse and the 9th Lancers, and a wild stampede resulted. The rest of the British cavalry, seeking revenge for the hurt suffered at Chillianwallah, joined in to shatter the enemy horsemen, riding on and over Sikh infantry, capturing guns and wagons, turning the enemy into a mass of fugitives.

The pursuing troopers did not draw rein until they had ridden 15 miles beyond Gujerat, by which time the Sikh army was completely wrecked, deprived of its camp, its colours, and 53 guns. Thus was the Punjab annexed to the British Empire after the hardest fighting the British had ever known in India. The Sikhs laid down their arms with dignity, acknowledging the martial supremacy of the British and in the ensuing years were proud to fight under the banner of the Empress Queen.

The Indian Mutiny that broke out in 1857 came as a great shock to the

Types of the 6th Bombay Cavalry or Jacob's Horse, founded by Brigadier John Jacob, whom Sir Charles Napier called the 'Seydlitz of the Sind Army'.

Tent-pegging was another popular cavalry sport and demonstration of lance-wielding skill.

164

165

British. The sepoy army had loyally served the East India Company for more than a century. In 1857 the Company's Army contained about 40,000 British soldiers and some 30,000 sepoys commanded by white officers. For various reasons discontent rose in the Bengal Native Army, in particular, and discipline deteriorated. The final straw was the introduction of a new cartridge said to be greased with a mixture of beef-fat and pig's lard – a religious abomination to both Hindus and Muslims – giving rise to the rumour that the British planned to first pollute then Christianise the sepoys. On 10 May 1857 the native garrison at Meerut mutinied, killed their white officers, massacred the Europeans, and marched on Delhi, ancient capital of the Mogul Empire. They occupied it, murdered every European and Christian they could find and proclaimed the old King of Delhi as Emperor of Hindustan.

Other mutinies swiftly followed and what had started as a purely military revolt took on a wider front as many Indian potentates seized the

Hunting wild boar with the lance. Pig-sticking was a popular sport with cavalrymen in India.

Bengal Cavalry capturing a retreating train after the battle of Tel-el-Kebir in September 1882.

chance to regain lost power. The principal centres of operations were Delhi, Cawnpore and Lucknow, the latter places being held by small British garrisons besieged by rebels. Not all the native regiments mutinied. The Madras Army was little touched by the storm: the Madras, Bombay and Hyderabad armies played an active role in suppressing mutiny and rebellion in various parts of India, notably in central India. The fidelity of the Sikhs of the Punjab Irregular Force added to the steady loyalty of most of the Bombay and Madras corps enabled the British to reconquer Hindustan. Many regiments whose loyalty was suspect were disbanded early in the upheaval.

Among the irregular corps that came to fame in the Mutiny were Hodson's Horse, Wales's Horse, Lind's Horse, Cureton's Multanis, the Mahratta Horse, the Sikh Irregular Cavalry, the Delhi Pioneers, the Sikh Volunteer Infantry, and 18 regiments of Punjab Infantry. Four regiments of white cavalry were formed in 1858 to replace eight regiments of mutinous Bengal light cavalry: after the Mutiny these were transferred to the regular British Army as hussar regiments.

William Hodson, born in 1821, was educated at Rugby and Trinity College, Cambridge. At the age of 24 he joined the 2nd Bengal Grenadiers and served in the First Sikh War. In 1847 he became second-in-command

Camp of the 13th Bengal Lancers during the campaign in Egypt of 1882, showing *sowars* feeding the horses.

and adjutant of the Corps of Guides, a body raised in 1846 by Lieutenant Harry Lumsden, its first commander, for general service as well as in the capacity indicated by their name. The Guides consisted of both cavalry and infantry. Lumsden recruited men 'from every wild and warlike tribe... men notorious for desperate deeds, leaders of forays, who kept the passes into the hills, and lived amid inaccessible rocks. He made Guides of them.'

Lumsden is also notable in military history for introducing khaki dress. 'Discarding the conspicuous scarlet of the old-time Indian regiments, Lumsden dressed his men in khaki – the first corps to be clothed in uniform of this colour. The clothing of the Guides was dyed by men regimentally employed.' The word 'khaki' is Persian meaning 'dust-coloured'. The dye used was known as *multani mati*, meaning 'earth of Multan'. Not surprisingly the Guides were soon nicknamed 'The Mudlarks'. The celebrated General 'Sam' Browne was an officer in the Guides. He won the Victoria Cross during the Indian Mutiny when, with one *sowar*, he charged a rebel nine-pounder at Seerporah in August 1858 and prevented it being

A *dafadar* (sergeant) of the 1st Bengal Cavalry in the 1890s. First raised in 1803 by James Skinner, the 1st Irregular Cavalry or Skinner's Horse remained loyal during the Indian Mutiny and in 1860 was taken into the Queen's service as the senior cavalry regiment of the Bengal army, becoming the 1st Bengal Cavalry.

reloaded to fire on British infantry. In the close combat Browne received a severe sword-cut on the left knee, and his left arm was sliced through at the shoulder. He lost the arm, and because he could not easily draw his sword from its scabbard, he designed a special sword-belt and pistol-harness – the so-called Sam Browne belt – later adopted by officers all over the world.

Hodson took command of the Guides in 1852 and in 1857 was com-

missioned to raise and lead 'a corps of Irregular Horse on the usual rates of pay and regular complement of native officers'. Hodson's Horse soon won a reputation: 'Their rapidity of movement and dashing courage made them a terror to the rebels.' Hodson met his death in March 1858 during the final taking of Lucknow. Major Elliott, who recorded the deeds of native soldiers, described the following incident in which two members of Hodson's Horse were involved during the siege of Lucknow.

'Two gallant Sikh *sowars* rode up, one of whom at once attacked the Daroga [rebel leader]; his companion tackled another. A tremendous blow straight down upon the Sikh's left shoulder was delivered by the Daroga with such force that, received as it was by the *sowar* upon his shield, it made him reel in his saddle. A sweeping return cut was given by the Sikh at the Daroga's head, but he sprang away and aimed a stroke at the *sowar's* side. This the Sikh parried with his sword, and then, finding he was at a disadvantage by fighting on horseback, he flung himself from the saddle and rushed at the maddened Daroga. Another well-aimed blow by the infuriated rebel, which would have cleft the *sowar's* skull, was received upon his shield; yet such was the force that it sent him backwards to the ground; but springing to his feet before the Daroga could get at him, he renewed the combat. Once more the Sikh was struck down, his life being saved again by his trusty shield. Thrice he was dashed to the earth, from which he sprang up with rapidity, or he

170

The Governor-General's Bodyguard, Calcutta, painted by H. Bunnett, 1888.

would have been slain. On the last occasion, quickly rising from the prostrate position, he made a desperate effort to end the combat. He leaped well to the left, and as he did so he gave a sweeping backward cut at his adversary's head. The Daroga with the quickness of lightning saw his danger, and jumped to avoid the blow, but the keen edge of the *sowar*'s *tulwar* near its point reached the back of his opponent's neck. The Daroga staggered to the ground, his head fell forward, and he was instantly despatched by a well-directed point from his Sikh antagonist. Whilst this was going on a similar combat took place between the other Sikh and the remaining enemy; this *sowar* also succeeded in killing his man.'

171

After the Mutiny was put down the government of India was transferred to the Crown and the European regiments of the East India Company were absorbed into the British Army: for example, the 3rd Bengal European Cavalry became the 21st Hussars, and in 1897 became the 21st Lancers, under which title the regiment made its famous charge at Omdurman in 1898. In 1861 the native regiments were reorganised into the Indian Army and given new titles and numbers. The 1st and 2nd Hodson's Horse, for example, became the 9th and 10th Bengal Cavalry, and later these particular regiments were designated Bengal Lancers.

With a few exceptions Indian Army cavalry regiments were organised on the *silladar* system mentioned earlier, and consisted of 'class regiments' or 'class squadron' regiments, the former being composed entirely of men of the same class (race or creed), the latter being formed of different class squadrons. The 14th Bengal Lancers, formerly known as Murray's Jat Horse, was a class regiment composed exclusively of Jats. The 2nd Bengal Lancers (in 1897) was a class squadron regiment composed of four squadrons, one squadron of Sikhs, one of Rajputs, one of Jats, and one of Hindu Mahometans.

Indian Army cavalry, officered by natives and whites jointly, served with distinction in numerous British wars in various countries and campaigns on the rugged North-West of India. Regiments saw active service in China in 1860 and during the Boxer Rebellion of 1900; in Abyssinia, 1868; the

Guard tent of the Mysore Lancers, India, circa 1896.

Afghan War of 1878–80; in Egypt, 1882; and the Sudan in 1884–85. Several Punjab cavalry regiments served in the Afghan War mentioned and Major Ashe, who was there, recorded his impressions of the 3rd Punjab Cavalry:

'Arms, horse equipment, saddlery, uniform, and drill are excellent, and even our own cavalry might take an occasional hint from the system employed by these turbaned spearmen. Formerly the *sowar* carried a pistol in his wallet, but now these are available for spare kit or provisions, as a beneficent Government issues to him a Snider carbine! In addition to this weapon he carries a curved and uncommonly sharp sword and lance. His uniform consists of a dark-blue *bunghi*, or turban, wound deftly round a red wadded skull-cap; his frock, or *koorta*, of coarse blue serge, shaped something like a Norfolk shirt, and bound into the waist by a red cummerbund; wide, yellow pyjamas tucked into long boots of brown untanned leather; brown leather pouch and sword-belt, the former carrying 20 rounds, and a very long bamboo lance with bright steel point and blue and white pennon... The *sowar* would, of course, be incomplete without his *choga* (cloak) and this he carries strapped over his wallet, while he has a lance-socket at each stirrup, a grain-bag on the near side behind the saddle, with the horse's blanket and pegs fastened behind. On the off-side is the carbine in its bucket, as also his shot-case. These men are, for this country, the perfection of Light Cavalry.'

During the Egyptian War of 1882 the 13th Bengal Cavalry carried out daring reconnaissance and escort duties. The regiment distinguished itself

173

Spahi, the colourful light cavalry of French-controlled Algeria, shown in a spirited charge against hostile tribesmen. An illustration of 1888.

in warning the British force of a second Egyptian attack on Kassassin. 'Our troops were very nearly being surprised,' writes Grant in his history of the war.

'For the first intimation that General Graham had of the coming attack was when Colonel Pennington, of the 13th Bengal Lancers, rode out at five in the morning to post vedettes, and found himself, to his astonishment, in the presence of three squadrons of cavalry and a column of infantry, advancing in regular attack formation. The cavalry were coming on, firing from their saddles as usual, and making no attempt to charge. Through the misty morning air a second and stronger line of cavalry could be observed advancing... Sending two of his lancers back to camp at a gallop to give warning of the approaching attack, Colonel Pennington, with great coolness and judgement, dismounted his remaining 28 men and opened fire from behind a sandy ridge. The hostile cavalry continued to advance steadily, and eventually surrounded him, on which he gave the order to mount and charge home to the British camp. His lancers did so gallantly, with the loss of only one, while under the lance or *tulwar* ten Egyptians fell in the dust; and thanks to his cool

Maharajah Sir Pertab Singh, a distinguished cavalry officer. Colonel of the Jodhpur Lancers, he served in Europe with the Indian Army in World War 1.

Bengal Lancers charging German infantry on the Western Front early in World War 1. A romanticised illustration by Christopher Clark and reproduced in *The Sphere* of 19 December 1914.

courage, and the promptitude of other cavalry and mounted men, the infantry and artillery had time to form line of battle [and beat off the enemy attack].'

Indian Army regiments served gallantly in the various theatres of World War 1. Over one million Indian soldiers served between 1914 and 1918, including 15 cavalry regiments; they saw action against the Germans on the Western Front and against the Turks in the Middle East. The first officer of the Indian Army to win the Victoria Cross in France was Lieutenant Frank Alexander de Pass of the 34th Prince Albert Victor's Own Poona Horse, during a dismounted action at Festubert in November 1914; his was a posthumous award. Lance *Daffadar* (Corporal) Gobind Singh of the 28th Light Cavalry, attached to the 2nd Lancers (Gardner's Horse), won his VC in France for action in December 1917. He volunteered three times to carry messages between the regiment and brigade headquarters, a distance of a mile and a half, over open ground which was under observation and heavy fire of the enemy. He delivered his messages, although on each of the three occasions his horse was shot under him and he continued on foot.

In Palestine, September 1918, *Ressaidar* (Troop commander) Badlu Singh of the 14th Lancers, attached to the 29th Lancers (Deccan Horse), won a posthumous VC when his squadron was ordered to charge a strong Turkish position. Badlu's men were suffering casualties from machine-guns and infantry fire situated on a small hill to the left front. Without hesitation, Badlu detailed six *sowars* to follow him and they charged and took the machine-guns and captured the infantry. The Sikh officer gave his life in order to save his squadron heavy casualties.

It is appropriate to end this chapter with the story of Captain Arthur

Sandeman who led one of the last cavalry charges in World War 2. Sandeman loved horses and learned to ride at a young age. He joined the army in the period between the World Wars, at a time when mechanisation was swiftly replacing the horse in cavalry regiments. He went to India and joined one of the few mounted regiments that remained in the British Army, King George V's Own Central India Horse, and enjoyed the traditional cavalry sports of polo and hunting the wild pig with a spear from horseback. Sandeman, or 'Sandy' as he was known to his brother officers, quickly gained a reputation as an eccentric, for he adopted the style and manner of a cavalryman of the late Victorian age. Sandeman was, it seems, born out of his time. 'All his ideas centred around an earlier period,' records the historian of the Central India Horse, 'and the spruce figure of Sandy, faultlessly attired in the costume of half a century ago, driving about the cantonments in a horse buggy, was one that was quaint, even startling.'

When World War 2 broke out in 1939 the Central India Horse was mechanised and by the end of 1941 all cavalry regiments in the British and Indian armies had been remounted on armoured vehicles. Because of his passion for horse and dislike of motor and armoured vehicles, Sandy transferred to the Burma Frontier Force (a para-military force formed from the Burma Military Police in 1937) that contained both cavalry and infantry units. When the Japanese invaded Burma, Sandeman and his *sowars* scouted against the advancing enemy. On 21 March 1942 Sandeman's squadron was part of the allied force of Chinese, British and Americans defending Toungoo airfield in central Burma.

177

The 20th Deccan Horse. On 14 July 1916 a squadron of this regiment with a squadron of the 7th Dragoon Guards was ordered to attempt a breakthrough at High Wood in the battle of Albert. They failed to break through and suffered heavy casualties.

On this day, 21 March, James Lunt, as he describes in his book *Charge to Glory!*, was sitting in a stationary train a few miles outside Toungoo when 'Sandy Sandeman rode by with his troopers earlier this morning; they are carrying out a reconnaissance towards Sittang, he says... He also told me he was riding the best polo pony in Burma... He moved off with his column about nine o'cock – about sixty of them, and nearly all Sikhs.'

On approaching the airfield, Sandeman observed through his binoculars a large force of troops advancing over the flat terrain. He was not sure whether they were Chinese or Japanese, for both wore similar uniforms. As he and his troopers trotted closer to investigate they rode into a Japanese ambush. With bullets flying at him, Sandeman's immediate reaction was instinctive to one imbued with the cavalry spirit. He drew his sabre, ordered his trumpeter to sound the charge, and dashed straight at the enemy with his Sikhs right behind him. Sandeman was killed in the saddle. Only a handful of his *sowars* survived to tell the story of the heroic sun-helmeted sahib who died sword in hand riding at the gallop into the enemy.

178

6 · UNITED STATES CAVALRY

In January 1781 during the War of Independence Lord Cornwallis, the British commander in the South, ordered Lieutenant Colonel Banastre Tarleton, with 1,000 cavalry and infantry, to seek and destroy the rebel American force commanded by Brigadier General Daniel Morgan. Tarleton found Morgan at a place called the Cowpens in South Carolina. In numbers Morgan's force almost equalled that of Tarleton, but it was mostly militia and his cavalry was thought to be inferior to the British. A fine commander, Morgan decided to stand his ground and devised a plan. Tarleton, confident that he could smash the rebels, wasted no time in launching an attack.

Tarleton, 26 at the time, was a dashing and successful leader of light cavalry. He first saw action at Charleston in June 1776 and his merit soon gained him promotion to Brigade-Major of Cavalry. He was next selected to be Lieutenant Colonel Commandant of the newly-raised British Legion, a force of loyalist Americans formed round a cadre of British troops. The cadre of the Legion's cavalry section was drawn from the 17th Light Dragoons. Only two British cavalry regiments served in America during the war – the 16th and 17th Light Dragoons.

Tarleton and his green-coated Legion horsemen became the scourge of the Carolinas, which proved ideal cavalry country. With a combination of speed, daring and tactical skill Tarleton secured some spectacular victories. In May 1780, after forcing his cavalry the remarkable distance of 105 miles in 54 hours, he caught up with 350 Virginians, under Colonel Abraham Buford, who were marching to help the garrison of besieged Charleston. Tarleton fell on Buford's force at the Waxhaws, a district near the North Carolina border, and took the rebels by surprise with a sudden charge, slaughtering most of them and refusing to honour the white flag displayed by Buford.

In August, following Cornwallis's defeat of the rebel force commanded by General Gates at Camden, Tarleton's implacable cavalry pursued the fleeing Americans for 30 miles, killing most of those who lagged in their flight. A few days later Tarleton destroyed a force under General Sumter at Fishing Creek. Because of his ruthless lack of mercy, the rebels called him 'Bloody Tarleton'. Now, at Cowpens, he intended to annihilate Daniel Morgan and his men.

Morgan, of Welsh immigrant blood and a cousin to Daniel Boone, had served the British army as a horse teamster and in 1756, having struck a

General Sir Banastre Tarleton painted by Sir Joshua Reynolds in 1782. He is wearing the uniform of the British Legion with the 'Tarleton helmet' he made popular – a peaked leather cap with a fur crest.

The battle of Cowpens in 1781 depicting the action in which Lieutenant-Colonel William Washington came under direct attack by Tarleton and two officers. Washington was saved by Trumpeter Collins, seen on the left firing a pistol, and Sergeant-Major Perry on the right.

British officer, was sentenced to 500 lashes. As a rebel commander the 'Old Waggoner,' as he was called, had several victories to his credit. His force at Cowpens was largely militia – men who fought battles and then went home – stiffened by units of the Continental Army, trained soldiers enlisted for the duration of the war. Morgan's detachment of cavalry – the 3rd Continental Light Dragoons – was commanded by Lieutenant Colonel William Washington.

Fully understanding the limitations of his poorly disciplined militia, Morgan deployed them to full advantage. He selected a hill as the centre of his position and formed his main line of Continental infantry on it, deliberately leaving his flanks open (a dangerous thing to do). Well forward of the main line he placed his militia in two widely separated ranks, instructing the first line to fire two volleys then fall back on the second line, the combined line to fire until pressed by the enemy, then to fall back to the rear of the Continentals and re-form as a reserve. Behind the hill he placed the cavalry, ready to charge the attacking British at the critical moment. Morgan informed every man of his plan of battle and what was expected of him.

As the redcoat infantry advanced in regular formation they were checked by the militia riflemen, then took the retreat of the two lines as the

181

beginning of a rout and rushed headlong into the steady, withering fire of
the Continentals on the hill. With the British well advanced and in
disorder, Morgan launched his waiting cavalry at the enemy's right flank,
and the re-formed militia struck the British left. Caught in a clever double
envelopment, the British could not stop Washington's 80 dragoons from
cutting right through to Tarleton's reserve, the 200 troopers of the British
Legion.

In the slashing fight that ensued, Washington's sword broke off at the
hilt. Attacked by three officers, including Tarleton, he was saved by
Sergeant Major Perry who arrived just in time to parry the blow and
disable the sword-arm of one of the officers as he swung his sabre to cut
down Washington. A young American trumpeter named Collins, too frail
to wield a sword, brought down another of the officers with a pistol shot.
Tarleton himself managed to escape unscathed, but not before he had shot

at Washington and injured his knee. In Tarleton's own words it was a
'decisive rout'. Out of his force of 1,000 he left behind 600 as prisoners,
100 dead on the field, his two guns, his colours, 800 muskets, 100 dragoon
horses, and a large part of his baggage train.

Morgan's generalship had saved the day and the infant 3rd Continental
Light Dragoons, raised in 1777, had won their spurs in ensuring victory by
defeating a bigger and more experienced cavalry force. The Continental
Army was composed mainly of infantry and artillery, with very little
cavalry. The cavalry tradition of the US army dates from March 1777 when
Congress approved the organisation of four cavalry regiments proposed by
General George Washington, the commander-in-chief. Washington had
written to Congress in December 1776: 'From the experience of the utility
of Horse, I am convinced there is no carrying on the War without them,

184

and I would therefore recommend the establishment of one or more
Corps.'

In his *Military Guide for Young Officers*, published in Philadelphia in 1775,
Thomas Simes gives the following uses for which light cavalry should be
employed:

'In reconnoitering the enemy and discovering his motions... they are also on such
expeditions to avoid engaging the enemy... to be made use of for distant advanced
posts to prevent the army from being falsely alarmed and surprised... small patrols
to be kept going around the army to prevent desertion. Parties are also to be sent
out to distress the enemy by depriving them of forage and provisions, by surprising
their convoys, attacking their baggage, harrassing them on the march, cutting off
small detachments, and sometimes carrying off foraging parties. Light cavalry are
moreover to be employed in raising contributions, and when the army marches
they may compose the advance guard, and when other troops cannot be spared,
they may form the rear guards or cover the baggage.'

The new cavalry regiments authorised by Congress were based on light
horse militia and numbered 1st, 2nd, 3rd and 4th Continental Light
Dragoons; a dragoon being trained to fight on horse and on foot with a

186

Charge of the US 2nd Dragoons at the Mexican guns in the battle of Resaca de la Palma in May 1846. Painted by Hal Stone.

carbine. Because of the shortage of horses and suitable recruits these regiments were always under strength, and, like the British cavalry, were mostly used in the South. In September 1777 the Polish soldier of fortune Count Casimir Pulaski was made commander of the Corps of Continental Dragoons, an appointment that caused resentment among the native American officers. Pulaski's career, however, was curtailed: he was killed in October 1779 while recklessly charging a British redoubt at Savannah.

As a matter of interest the French military contribution to the American cause in the war included 280 hussars of the Volontaires Etrangers de Lauzun of the force commanded by the Comte de Rochambeau. These hussars took part in the battles of York River and won fame at the siege of Gloucester against Tarleton. After Rochambeau's departure, the hussars served under Washington's direct orders until 1783.

Captain Henry Lee of the 1st Continental Light Dragoons distinguished himself from the moment he first went into action and in July 1779, aged 23, he commanded his own Legion – Lee's Legion – a force of light horse and light infantry. He gained the nickname 'Light-Horse Harry.' His son, Robert E. Lee, born in 1807, was destined to lead the Confederate forces in the Civil War of 1861-65. In April 1781 'Light-Horse Harry' Lee was sent to

LINCOLN CAVALRY

Col. ANDREW T. McREYNOLDS, Commanding.

WANTED
A FEW GOOD MEN!

To be in the field by 4th of July, if possible, who can furnish their own horses and equipments.

"EXTRACT FROM OFFICIAL ORDERS."

The allowances for Clothing for Cavalry, shall be $3 50 per month. Each Officer, Non-commisioned Officer, Private, and Musician, shall furnish his own Horse and Horse Equipments. [Equipments and Clothing can be furnished for $50] In case the Horse is lost in action, the Government pays for same 50 Cents a day is allowed for use of Horse.

Some good **FARRIERS** and **BLACKSMITHS**, wanted for the above Regiment, PAY EXTRA.

This is the only Cavalry Regiment accepted by the United States Government for immediate Service, and to serve during the War.

☞Apply immediately to Head Quarters,

403 Walnut Street, Phila., or to William H. Boyd, Box 661 Post Office.

Recruiting poster for Volunteer Cavalry in the Mexican War of 1846-48.

General James Ewell Brown ('Jeb') Stuart, celebrated commander of Confederate cavalry who died in the Civil War.

join Francis Marion, another rebel cavalry leader of note known as the 'Swamp Fox'. Marion and his irregular horsemen waged a successful guerrilla war against the British in the South. Emerging from the swampland, he and his mounted marauders attacked isolated enemy garrisons, inspiring them with dread of 'that damned swamp fox'. Moving swiftly from point to point he would fall suddenly on the enemy and fought with a ferocity and ruthlessness that equalled Tarleton.

Colonel William Washington was given command of the 3rd Continental Light Dragoons and at the battle of Guilford Courthouse, 15 March 1781, his regiment galloped to the rescue of the Fifth Maryland Regiment, whose raw troops had been thrown into retreat by a furious assault of the British

Foot Guards. It was a critical moment. The American dragoons halted the advance and drove the guards back. In the battle of Eutaw Springs in September 1781, Washington was sent to attack the rear of a reserve battalion of grenadiers and light infantry. In attempting this ill-conceived manoeuvre, Washington's horsemen were impeded by dense undergrowth, the while struggling through under heavy musket fire. Washington's mount was shot under him, and, entangled in the stirrups, he was wounded and captured. Most of his dragoons were either killed or wounded.

At the war's end (which came into effect formally in late January 1783) the dragoon regiments were disbanded and the Continental Army replaced with a small Regular Army composed of infantry and artillery, a force necessary in the words of George Washington 'to awe the Indians, protect our Trade, prevent the encroachment of our Neighbours of Canada and the Floridas, and guard us at least from surprises; also for security of our magazines'. Washington recommended a force of four regiments of infantry and one of artillery totalling 2,630 officers and men. Having won freedom from Britain the young republic now faced a serious security problem in the West where the settlers demanded protection against the hostile Indians.

Although Washington had not recommended a cavalry force for the regular army, General Harmar, having returned from an ill-starred expedition in 1790 against the tribesmen, opined that 'without a regular

Lieutenant-General Nathan B. Forrest of the Confederate army, a master of irregular cavalry operations.

General Philip Sheridan (far left) in war conference with his officers, including George A. Custer (seated far right). Photograph attributed to Mathew Brady.

cavalry I know not how the Indians can ever be effectually checked'. After another disastrous march against the Indians in 1791, led by General Arthur St Clair, President Washington appointed Major General Anthony Wayne to command and train a Legion of the United States, composed of regular infantry, and light dragoons. Wayne whipped the Legion into shape and, reinforced by mounted militia in July 1794, he led some 3,000 men into the battle of Fallen Timbers and routed a force of 1,000 Indians.

In August 1795 the western tribes, their resistance broken, made peace and ceded their Ohio lands to the United States. In 1797 Congress dropped the Legion type of organisation and returned the regular army to the regimental pattern, with four regiments of infantry, a Corps of Artillery and Engineers, and two companies of light dragoons. By 1797 the entire force of dragoons were stationed along the southwest frontier. When the War of 1812 broke out between Britain and the United States, the 2nd US Light Dragoons came into being.

In the battle of the Thames on 5 October 1813 Brigadier General William Harrison led a force of 3,500 men against an allied Indian-British force of 2,900, of which some 900 were British regulars; the Indians were led by the great chief Tecumseh. Harrison's force included Colonel Richard Johnson's regiment of Kentucky Mounted Volunteers. Instead of attacking

191

with infantry in the traditional line-against-line fashion, Harrison ordered a mounted attack and Johnson's 500 Kentucky horsemen charged the British with such vigour and violence that the redcoats and redskins were routed, Johnson himself killing Tecumseh.

When the war ended in February 1815, Congress decided to abolish the regular dragoons and the US Army lacked a regular cavalry until 1833 when the US Regiment of Dragoons was raised, commanded by Colonel Henry Dodge. The dragoons patrolled the Great Plains, campaigned against the Indians and escorted caravans on the Santa Fe Trail. In 1836 Congress opened its tight fiscal purse and created the 2nd Regiment of US Dragoons. In the war with Mexico (1846–48) a regiment of mounted riflemen was added to the regular army. In the battle of Resaca de la Palma, General Zachary Taylor ordered Captain Charles May and his company of 2nd US Dragoons to charge and take a battery of Mexican guns that was causing him great concern; despite the military dictum that cavalry should never charge artillery, the guns were a problem that had to be removed, at whatever sacrifice. Here is a contemporary account of the charge:

'Instantly the squadron of dragoons sprang forward, May in the advance, with his long hair streaming behind like the rays of a comet. The earth shook beneath the iron hoofs of their steeds, and the rays of the tropic sun flashed back in flame from their burnished sabres, as they swept along, cheered by a shout of exultation from the artillery and infantry. Still foremost, May reached at length the batteries in the road and as his steed rose upon the enemy's breastworks, he turned to wave on his men to the charge. Closely pressing upon him was Lieutenant Inge, who, in like manner turned to encourage his platoon, when a terrible discharge of grape and canister from the upper battery swept down upon them and dashed to the earth, in mangled and bloody masses, 18 horses and 7 men, among them the gallant Inge and his charger. May's steed at a bound cleared the batteries, followed by Lieutenant Stevens and the survivors of the 1st and 2nd platoons. Their impetus carried them through and beyond the batteries, when charging back, they drove the enemy from the guns and silenced their fire. Captain Graham and Lieutenants Winship and Pleasonton, with the 3rd and 4th platoons, in the mean time swept to the left of the road and at the point of the sword carried the battery situated there.'

The dragoons had suffered such heavy casualties that, having silenced the guns, they could not hold them and infantry went forward to complete the task. Captain May had behaved with signal bravery, in this his first charge in war, but he somewhat sullied his guidon by claiming to have personally captured General Diaz de la Vega. For this he was promoted and hailed as a national hero. The truth of the matter was, however, that May's bugler had in fact taken General Vega and May seized upon the opportunity for self-glorification. Dragoons who knew the real story despised May for his misrepresentation of the action.

The Mexican regular army in this war included 15 infantry regiments, 4 artillery brigades and 15 cavalry regiments. The smartly uniformed Mexican light cavalry, armed with the lance, carbine and sword, were particularly impressive. During the battle of Buena Vista, 22 February

Colonel John S. Mosby, another outstanding leader of Confederate horse. Herman Melville wrote of him: 'As glides in seas the shark/rides Mosby through green dark'.

192

Custer in action in September 1863 near Culpeper, Virginia, where his cavalry brigade captured three enemy guns. Custer's horse was killed by round shot which also wounded him in the leg and killed a trumpeter behind him. A contemporary engraving from *Frank Leslie's Illustrated Newspaper*.

1847, a brigade of Mexican lancers under General Torrejon threatened the American rear and were engaged by Arkansas and Kentucky mounted volunteers. In this clash of cavalry the Arkansas Colonel Yell received a lance point in the mouth that ripped away his jaw, and another in the chest that killed him. Torrejon's lancers did much execution until a squadron of the 1st Dragoons charged them, divided their ranks, and drove them into retreat.

The US won the war and imposed harsh terms on the conquered nation. The Rio Grande was established as the boundary of Texas, and New Mexico (including the present states of Arizona, New Mexico, Utah, Nevada, and parts of Wyoming and Colorado) and the present state of California were ceded to the US which, in return, agreed to pay Mexico the bargain price of 15 million dollars for the vast territories. General Taylor's victories served him well in his political aspirations. He was elected President of the United States in 1848.

Peace with Mexico brought an immediate reduction of the US army. The volunteers were discharged and sent home. The regiment of Mounted Riflemen was retained as part of the regular army but all the other new

193

General Sheridan leads his cavalry in a counterattack at Cedar Creek, October 1864, and snatches victory from the jaws of impending defeat. Lithograph by Kurz and Allison.

regiments, including the 3rd Dragoons, were disbanded. By the end of 1848 the regular army had reverted to peacetime strength and status (9,878 officers and enlisted men), but the Indian frontier remained a scene of constant unrest and active campaigns. In March 1855 Congress authorised four new regiments: the 1st and 2nd Cavalry and the 9th and 10th Infantry regiments. The mounted arm thus consisted of dragoons, mounted rifles, and cavalry until the Civil War, when the older names were discarded. All mounted regiments were then called cavalry and numbers were changed in accordance with regimental seniority.

American cavalry came of age in the Civil War. Both sides produced outstanding cavalry commanders. 'Jeb' Stuart, Nathan B. Forrest, John S. Mosby and John H. Morgan on the Confederate side. The Federal or Union forces produced Philip H. Sheridan, Benjamin H. Grierson, and a bunch of vigorous, ambitious and capable young officers, including George A. Custer, Ranald Mackenzie, Wesley Merritt and Judson Kilpatrick. James Ewell Brown ('Jeb') Stuart was a true cavalier son of the South, young and handsome, brave and audacious in action, flamboyant in dress, a much-admired, popular leader who inspired his men with his own enthusiasm and confidence. Together with Robert E. Lee, Stuart personified all that was best in Southern gentry.

194

Sheridan leads the decisive cavalry charge at Five Forks, Virginia, April 1865, in which Robert E. Lee was finally defeated. Lithograph by Kurz and Allison.

Born in Virginia in 1833 and West Point trained, Jeb Stuart was commissioned into the US Mounted Rifles in 1854. Transferring to the 1st Cavalry he spent five years on the frontier. When Virginia seceded from the Union he resigned from the US army and became a captain of cavalry in the Confederate forces and swiftly rose to command the 1st Virginia Cavalry. He distinguished himself in several major battles and in September 1861 was promoted brigadier general at the age of 29. Cavalry columns on both sides of the Civil War made deep penetration raids behind enemy lines to cause havoc and bring back prisoners, horses, and information.

On 13 June 1862 Jeb Stuart, with 1,200 cavalry, set out on a bold raid clear around the Federal lines, cutting telegraph wires, burning bridges, capturing wagons and supplies and, after an absence of two days, returned to Richmond (capital city of the Confederacy) with 165 prisoners and twice as many horses, having lost only one man. On the basis of Stuart's intelligence report Robert E. Lee attacked the Federal exposed right flank in the first of a series of battles known as the Seven Days' Campaign.

Cavalry raids sometimes secured vital documents from the enemy. In August 1862, prior to the battle of Second Bull Run, Jeb Stuart was nearly captured by Union cavalry. He escaped but his adjutant, who carried copies

of Lee's orders on him, was taken prisoner and the papers promptly forwarded to General Pope. Seeing that his position was dangerous, Pope withdrew the Army of Virginia to the north bank of the Rappahannock. Several days of feints and manoeuvres followed as Lee probed for openings across the fords of the river. Then, on the stormy night of 22 August Stuart crossed the river and managed to overrun Pope's tented headquarters in a lightning raid in which his men seized documents detailing Pope's deployment, and of reinforcements that were marching to join him. This information enabled Lee to plan his campaign in which he defeated General Pope.

A captain of cavalry, USA, during the Civil War, showing the McClellan-style saddle and method of wearing the sabre.

Major Albert G. Enos, 8th
Pennsylvania Cavalry regiment,
USA.

The broken and wooded terrain of most battles proved poor country for
concerted mounted action and there were few grand cavalry against
cavalry encounters with drawn sabres – the greatest being at Brandy
Station in June 1863. With their superior speed and mobility cavalry on
both sides were employed in screening troop movements, reconnaissance,
and in advance guard actions in which they seized and held important
hills, river lines, and road and rail junctions pending the arrival of infantry.
Cavalrymen in this great war were dragoons in the proper sense: mounted
infantry who depended on firepower rather than sabre work. Armed with
sword, percussion-type revolver and breech-loading carbine they rode to

197

Cha's Schreyvogel

the scene of battle and fought on foot, often charging as infantry. The range and accuracy of rifles made it virtually impossible for horsemen to attack infantry in position.

Ulysses S. Grant, General-in-Chief of the Union Army, considered Nathan B. Forrest as 'about the ablest cavalry leader in the South... Forrest indeed performed the very remarkable feat of capturing, with cavalry, two gunboats and a number of transports, something the accomplishment of which is very hard to account for'. Forrest, a former dealer in horses and slaves, was a master of irregular cavalry. Uneducated in the military school he summed up the ingredients of victory as 'getting there fustest with the mostest'. His raiding and destruction caused the Federals much concern and tied up vital manpower in guard and escort duties. In April 1863 Forrest captured General Streight's entire Union cavalry brigade at Rome, Georgia, and won promotion to major general.

Grant held his own cavalry leader Philip Henry Sheridan in the highest regard, and rightly so; Sheridan served Grant and the Union extremely well. Born in 1831 he graduated from West Point in 1848 and became colonel of the 2nd Michigan Cavalry in 1862. 'He was in command at Booneville on 1 July [1862] with two small regiments,' Grant writes in his memoirs, 'when he was attacked by a force full three times as numerous as his own. By very skilful manoeuvres and boldness of attack he completely

'Custer's Last Stand' a detail of the painting by H. Charles McBarron.

199

routed the enemy. For this he was made a brigadier-general [of volunteers].'

Early in May 1864 Sheridan led 10,000 cavalry on a highly successful raiding operation towards Richmond, destroying stores, transport, railroads and rolling-stock. In the battle of Yellow Tavern, just outside Richmond, on 11 May the Union troopers clashed with Jeb Stuart's cavalry. The 4,500 Confederates were outnumbered and outfought, suffering some 1,000 casualties, including the mortally wounded Stuart, who died the following day in Richmond. In August 1864 Major General Sheridan was given command of the Army of the Shenandoah.

At Cedar Creek in October Sheridan's little army was taken by surprise by General Jubal Early and a Union defeat seemed certain. Sheridan was 20 miles away at Winchester, resting *en route* to join his army. On hearing the news, and the gunfire, Sheridan made his celebrated ride to the battlefield, where his dramatic appearance worked magic on his demoralized men. He rallied and re-formed them and turned impending defeat into a decisive victory. The cavalry charged and pursued the enemy for many miles, capturing 3 battle flags and 22 guns.

George Armstrong Custer was a favourite of Sheridan. Born in 1839 in

Ohio, Custer graduated from West Point in 1861 at the bottom of his class. The young lieutenant galloped into the war with an aggressive fighting spirit that soon brought him to the attention of his superiors. At the age of 23 he was made a brevet brigadier general, giving rise to his sobriquet the 'Boy General'. A born showman, he affected a flamboyant dress and manner. He wore his hair long in frontier style, his self-designed uniform consisted of a velvet jacket much ornamented with gold lace, a blue and white sailor shirt set off with a flowing crimson cravat, the lot topped by a wide-brimmed Western hat. From Gettysburg to Appomattox the gilded cavalier led first the Michigan Cavalry Brigade, his 'Wolverines', and then the Third Cavalry Division from one victory to another.

When the young Custer's command of the Michigan Brigade was questioned, General Pleasanton replied: 'Custer is the best cavalry general in the world and I have given him the best brigade.' A shameless seeker of glory, Custer's finest hour in the Civil War came in the pursuit of Lee's army from Richmond in April 1865, when his division held the van. By the end of the war Major General Custer was Phil Sheridan's trusted lieutenant and a national hero.

'The truth about Custer,' wrote an anonymous general in the *Cincinnati Commercial*, 'is that he was a pet soldier who had risen, not above his merit, but higher than

men of equal merit. He fought with Phil Sheridan, and through the patronage of Sheridan he rose, but while Sheridan liked his valor and dash, he never trusted his judgment. He was to Sheridan what Murat was to Napoleon... Rising to high command early in life, Custer lost the repose necessary to success in high command.'

Ranald Slidell Mackenzie was in character the complete opposite to Custer. Reserved in manner he eschewed personal glorification and no act of his ever brought censure from his superiors (unlike Custer, one of the most controversial soldiers in US history). Born in 1840 Mackenzie graduated from West Point top of his class of 1862. Starting his war service in the engineers, then artillery, he won promotion to brigadier general US Army and major general of volunteers. He commanded a highly efficient cavalry division during the Five-Forks-Appomattox campaign in the spring of 1865. General Grant in his memoirs said of him:

'I regarded Mackenzie as the most promising young officer in the army. Graduating at West Point, as he did, during the second year of the war, he had won his way up to the command of a corps [division] before its close. This he did upon his own merit and without influence.'

After the war both Mackenzie and Custer were to lead crack cavalry

203

regiments against hostile Indians of the West. The greatest cavalry battle of the war took place at Brandy Station, Virginia, on 9 June 1863, when Major General Pleasanton with 12,000 Union cavalry surprised Jeb Stuart's camp. For more than 12 hours some 20,000 troopers engaged in charging and sabre-swinging fights. In one part of the field the Union 6th Cavalry launched a charge against guns:

'It was made over a plateau fully 800 yards wide,' wrote Colonel Henderson of the Union army, who was there, 'and its objective point was the artillery at the church. Never rode troopers more gallantly than did those steady regulars, as, under a fire of shell and shrapnel and finally canister, they dashed up to the very muzzles, then through and beyond the guns. Here they were attacked from both sides and the survivors driven back.'

While Pleasanton drew back his horsemen to re-form and reorganize, two fresh Confederate regiments hit them in the left flank.

'This charge was as gallantly made and as gallantly met as any I have witnessed in nearly four years of active service,' Henderson commented. 'As the blue and grey riders mixed in the smoke and dust, minutes seemed to elapse before its effect was determined... and we saw that the field was won by the Confederates.'

204

Colonel Ranald Mackenzie, commander of the 4th Cavalry. Not as famous as Custer, his contemporary, Mackenzie campaigned successfully against the Plains Indians but did not seek out fame and glory.

Pleasanton retreated across the Rappahannock, having suffered more than 900 casualties. Stuart's losses amounted to 500 out of a force of 10,000.

In July 1866 the peacetime strength of the regular US army was set at 54,302 officers and enlisted men: 5 regiments of artillery, 45 of infantry, and 10 of cavalry (which included the newly raised cavalry regiments numbered 7 to 10), with provision for 1,000 Indian scouts. The army was reduced in 1869 and again in 1876 to a total force of 27,442. During the Indian Wars from 1865 to 1876 some 15,000 soldiers were stationed in the frontier West, scattered over a vast area in isolated forts. A garrison usually consisted of a company of infantry and a company of cavalry (after 1881 a cavalry company was designated a troop) but frequently a single company was the only protection for many miles of territory. In 1882 the troops of the entire 10 cavalry regiments were distributed among 55 posts in the Indian country.

A cavalry regiment rode, where it was possible, in columns of four and when dismounted for battle one man of each four would hold the horses while his comrades engaged in fighting. A fully complemented regiment of the 1870s numbered 940 officers and men, but regiments were usually understrength. Regulation cavalry uniform consisted of blue tunic and trousers with yellow piping and stripes, blue kepi or wide-brimmed campaign hat; however, on active service dress was varied, more for comfort than military correctness, and both officers and men wore a mixture of official and civilian dress, including buckskin, inspiring one observer to liken them to 'Bulgarian bandits'.

Patrolling and fighting on the cold Northern Plains or in the sunbaked Southwest was a difficult and dirty business and the cavalrymen developed into tough, experienced horse soldiers who were often required to ride for many miles a day on little food and rest, giving rise to the old cavalry boast 'Forty miles a day on beans and hay.' Troopers were armed with a sabre, revolver and carbine. They had little use for the sword. In 1873 the US Cavalry was issued with the new Colt Single Action .45 calibre revolver, a fine weapon indeed.

The 7th US Cavalry was raised in 1866 and George Armstrong Custer was assigned as second-in-command of the new regiment at Fort Riley, Kansas. After the Civil War when the volunteer army was disbanded and the regular army reorganised, Custer was appointed lieutenant colonel but as a matter of military courtesy and custom he was still addressed as 'general' as in former times. Because the two colonels appointed to command the 7th were permanently on detached service during Custer's time, he remained the active commander of the regiment until his death.

Custer's last fight, in the valley of the Little Bighorn River, Montana, 25 June 1876, is the most celebrated of the Indian wars. Its gunshots echo still in continuing historical controversy and many film versions. Contrary to popular belief the entire 7th Cavalry was not wiped out in the battle (it was not a massacre). Custer and his immediate command of some 225 men were all killed but the remainder of the regiment held out in a defensive

position until relieved by another column. The battle of the Little Bighorn was a single action in a concerted campaign involving three separate expeditions against the Sioux and Cheyenne. Custer's regiment, some 700 strong, was sent ahead of the main column to locate the encampment of the allied Indians. Custer had orders not to attack without support.

On finding the hostile village the impetuous Custer decided, perhaps, to cover himself with glory by attacking immediately, confident that his regiment alone could defeat the assembled warriors, the numbers of which have been estimated as about 3,000 to 4,000, although the figures are often disputed. In order to attack the encampment from different directions, Custer divided his regiment, and he and his detachment rode off to their doom. His movements after splitting from the regiment are shrouded in mystery. All that is known for fact is that he and his command, dismounted and surrounded, were overwhelmed by a great mass of warriors and all were killed. Elsewhere on the battlefield the remainder of the 7th lost nearly 100 men until rescued by the main column. Later the regiment was brought up to strength and continued in service.

After the disaster at Little Bighorn, Colonel Ranald Mackenzie and his crack 4th Cavalry took part in the large-scale operations against the Sioux and Cheyenne on the Northern Plains. In November 1876 Mackenzie defeated chief Dull Knife's Northern Cheyenne and destroyed their village. In the early 1870s Mackenzie and the 4th campaigned in Texas against the fierce Comanches and Kiowas. In September 1874 he found the winter camp of these hostiles in a last stronghold, the Palo Duro Canyon on the

Cavalry and infantry in full dress, 1888. Painted by H. A. Ogden.

Staked Plains. His surprise assault separated the Indians from their horses and supplies. While part of the 4th engaged the warriors, the others burned the *tipis* and the winter stores and drove off more than 1,000 horses, all of which Mackenzie then had slaughtered. Deprived of their precious horses and winter sustenance most of the hostiles were forced to surrender.

In 1879 Mackenzie campaigned successfully against the Ute tribe of Colorado. A ruthless, dedicated soldier who never spared himself in the field, Mackenzie did not seek out fame and glory; he never permitted journalists to accompany him on campaign, he never boasted of his triumphs, and he never wrote for publication; therefore it is not surprising that he did not achieve the celebrity of his contemporary the flamboyant Custer. In pursuit of his military objectives Mackenzie drove himself to breaking point. In March 1884 he was retired with the rank of brigadier general. He died insane at the age of 48 in January 1889.

The 19th century American public did not regard its regular army with much favour or esteem, the volunteer civilian turned soldier always being

A sergeant of cavalry drawn from life by Frederic Remington in 1890. Note the carbine attached to the shoulder belt. The sabre was little used in the Indian campaigns.

Henry O. Flipper, the first Negro graduate of West Point, served with the 10th Cavalry.

John J. Pershing, 2nd Lieutenant, 6th Cavalry, in 1887. At one time he headed a Negro cavalry regiment and gained the nickname 'Black Jack'. Pershing commanded the American forces in World War 1.

the hero of the non-militaristic American people. However, the Indian-fighting cavalry found a Rudyard Kipling-style champion in Thomas Edward Grafton who, in July 1899, had the following effort published in *Harper's New Monthly Magazine*:

TROOPER JACKSON.

'Don't you hear the bugle soundin', Trooper Jackson?
Come, shake yourself! There's trouble down ahead!
With a lot o'Texas rum they're a-makin' matters hum!
   She's a-tootin' 'boots an' saddles'! Out o' bed!
They're a-yellin' like the devil down the cañon!
A han'some lot of able-bodied Utes –
   An' the orders is, to rip 'em,
   An' to slash 'em, an' to nip 'em,
So jump along an' tumble in your boots!'

Oh! the ride was wild an' darin' down the bottom!
   Just sixty men, where ten troops should have been.
Not a tremble, not a quiver, as they dashed along the river
   At the howlin' horde of undiluted sin!
Like a teamster's whip the guidons were a-snappin'!
My God! the Indians numbered ten to one.
   Through the blindin' rifle flame
   They kept ridin' just the same,
With 'Old Glory' in the van a-leadin' on.

209

'On the Cavalry Drill Ground'. Illustration by Rufus F. Zogbaum in 1887.

'Cavalry – The Regimental Standard'. Illustration by Rufus F. Zogbaum. 1889.

Like a catapult they hit 'em in the middle!
  While the 'trader's' powder tore its dirty way;
An' the flamin' sheets o' hell scorched their tunics as they fell,
  An' their yellow plumes were crimson from the fray.
But the orders was to give 'em a 'chastisin' –
With sixty men, where ten troops should 'ave been.
  But they done it just the same!
  An' they never thought to blame,
With the forty dead and dyin' carried in.

  'Here's to you, cussin', fightin', Trooper Jackson!
  Here's to you for the glory that you won!
'Twas a slashin', dashin' ride when you crossed the Great Divide,
  But you done it as I like to see it done.
Your photograph's a-hangin' in the barrack,
An' your sabre ornaments the Colonel's hall.
  When your bugle sounded "taps",
  Then you won your shoulder-straps,
An' you'll wear 'em at the final grand "recall".'

Thomas Edward Grafton

The 9th and 10th US Cavalry regiments were raised in 1866 and were different in being Negro outfits led by white officers. The black cavalry took an active and distinguished part in a number of hard campaigns against the Sioux, Comanche and Apaches. They were highly regarded as fighters by the Indians who called them 'Buffalo Soldiers' because their short curly hair resembled that of the buffalo (the courage of which was much

respected by the Indians). The 10th accepted the sobriquet 'Buffalo
Soldiers' as an honour and adopted the animal as their regimental emblem.
Eleven Negro soldiers won the Medal of Honor for bravery in battle against
Indians. In 1878 Henry O. Flipper, the first Negro graduate from West
Point, became the first black officer to serve in the 10th. John J. Pershing
(later to become commanding general of US forces in France during World
War 1) served with the 10th and thereby gained his nickname 'Black Jack'.

The 10th Cavalry took part in the hunting down of Geronimo and his
fierce band of outlaw warriors in Arizona and Mexico. In May 1886 a troop
of the 10th commanded by Captain Lebo came upon Geronimo in the
Pinito Mountains of northern Sonora. In the ensuing fight the troop was
forced to pull back, leaving the badly wounded Corporal Scott out in the
open, an inviting target for Apache bullets. Then Lieutenant Clark, fresh
from West Point, braved the gunfire with a trooper and dashed out to bring
in the helpless man, an heroic incident immortalised by the Western artist
Frederic Remington in his illustration 'The Rescue of Corporal Scott' for
Harper's Weekly of 21 August 1886. Remington rode with the 10th Cavalry
across the Arizona desert and wrote about, and illustrated, his experience
in *A Scout with the Buffalo Soldiers* published in *Century Magazine*, April 1889:

'Together at the head of the little cavalcade rode the lieutenant and I, while behind,
in single file, came the five troopers, sitting loosely in their saddles with the long
stirrup of the United States cavalry seat, forage-hats set well over the eyes, and
carbine, canteens, saddle-pockets, and lariats, rattling at their sides. Strung out
behind were the four pack-mules... The sun was getting higher in the heavens

211

'The Rescue of Corporal Scott' of the 10th (Negro) Cavalry during the Geronimo campaign, as described in the main text. This illustration by Frederic Remington was published in *Harper's Weekly* 21 August 1886.

Theodore Roosevelt as Lieutenant-Colonel of the First US Volunteer Cavalry – the famous Rough Riders – in 1898.

and began to assert its full strength... The water in my canteen was hot and tasteless, and the barrel of my carbine, which I touched with my ungloved hand, was so heated that I quickly withdrew it... the horses moved along with downcast heads. The men wore a solemn look as they rode along, and now and then one would nod as though giving over to sleep... The great clouds of dust choke you and settle over horse, soldier, and accouterments until all local color is lost and black man and white man wear a common hue.'

The Spanish-American War of 1898 was welcomed by most Americans who, primed, prodded and misinformed by the popular Press and agitated by bellicose politicians like Theodore Roosevelt, regarded armed intervention in Cuba as a noble action in which they could kick the oppressive Spaniards out of the island and free the Cubans from colonial rule. To the ambitious Roosevelt, physically brave and brim-full of energy, the war

presented a splendid opportunity for him to win military glory in the field. So when Congress authorised recruitment of three volunteer cavalry regiments in the West and Southwest, Roosevelt immediately offered to raise and command one of them. He had spent some years out West in the 1880s as a cattle rancher and had a great admiration for the self-reliant cowboy type.

The 1st US Volunteer Cavalry was recruited principally from Arizona, New Mexico, Texas, and the Indian Country (Oklahoma). Roosevelt, owing to his lack of military experience had the good sense to refuse the colonelcy of the regiment, suggesting that his friend Leonard Wood, an

214

'A Cavalry Breakfast on the Plains' painted by Remington circa 1890. These tough horsemen claimed they could travel '40 miles a day on beans and hay'.

experienced soldier, be made colonel while he served as second in command. Newspapers promptly dubbed the outfit the 'Rough Riders' and the regiment came to officially adopt the term. They were also known as 'Teddy's Terrors'. Roosevelt was pleased with his men's martial appearance. 'Their uniform suited them,' he wrote. 'In their slouch hats, blue flannel shirts, brown trousers, leggings and boots, with handkerchiefs knotted loosely around their necks, they look exactly as a body of cowboy cavalry should look.'

The embarkation for Cuba, at Tampa, Florida, was chaotic to say the least. It took four days to embark the army of some 17,000, an operation which if properly organised could have been done in eight hours. This was typical of the lack of planning that plagued the US army, unprepared as it was for a foreign campaign, throughout the war. Because of a shortage of transport ships Roosevelt's Rough Riders had to leave four Troops behind, and all the horses of the other ranks. Only the officers' mounts were taken to Cuba. Roosevelt's two horses were accompanied by his Negro servant, Marshall, an old 'buffalo soldier' of the 9th Cavalry. In Cuba, Colonel Wood took charge of a brigade and Teddy was left in full command of the Rough Riders.

On 1 July the regiment took part in the famous action to secure the San Juan heights, a fortified ridge in front of Santiago. General Shafter ordered a frontal attack. This was Roosevelt's 'crowded hour'. On horseback, fully exposed to heavy fire, he led his dismounted Rough Riders, and various

215

units of other regiments (including the Negro 9th and 10th Cavalry) up Kettle Hill, a height separate from the main ridge. The troopers stormed the hill and captured it. Almost overnight Roosevelt became a national hero and his Rough Riders shared the fame; the war was well covered by reporters in the field.

Two weeks after the successful assault on the San Juan hills the Spanish surrendered Santiago. In August Spain agreed to get out of Cuba and the war was virtually over. The Rough Riders were shipped home in early August 1898 and disbanded in September. Theodore Roosevelt, riding high on his war record, went on to become Governor of New York, was elected Vice-President of the United States in 1900, and succeeded the assassinated McKinley the following year, remaining in office till 1909. As a result of the Spanish-American War the US government decided to annex the Philippines, a former Spanish possession, and the US army found itself fighting a nationalist Filipino force under Don Emilio Aguinaldo. Nine regiments of US cavalry saw active service in the Philippines between 1899 and 1901.

In July 1901 Congress authorised five new regiments of regular cavalry – the 11th, 12th, 13th, 14th and 15th – and by 1916 the US cavalry had a strength of 15,424. The Mexican Civil War of 1910–20 created a number of border incidents with the US. The most serious, the raid on Columbus, New Mexico, by Pancho Villa and his irregular horsemen, nearly triggered war between the nations. Francisco 'Pancho' Villa, a mercurial former bandit and guerrilla general, attacked Columbus on 9 March 1916, in an apparent fit of pique having lost the sympathy and support of the US government in his political ambitions. His 500 yelling, shooting raiders clattered through the border town and killed 18 Americans before being driven across the frontier by troopers of the 13th Cavalry.

President Woodrow Wilson immediately sent Brigadier General 'Black Jack' Pershing with a punitive expedition into Mexico 'with the sole object of capturing Villa and preventing further raids by his band'. This was done with the nod from the Mexican government. Divided into three brigades, the punitive expedition included the 7th, 10th, 11th and 13th Cavalry plus infantry and artillery, totalling some 5,000 regulars. Pershing never caught Villa but he did punish his guerrillas and put a stop to cross-border raids. The Punitive Expedition killed, wounded and captured some 500 Villistas before clashes between his troops and government soldiers, and growing protestations of 'invasion' by the Mexican government, brought about Pershing's withdrawal.

Pershing's mounted pursuit of Villa into Mexico was in reality the swan song of the US cavalry in its traditional role: the regular army's final major use of horse soldiers. When America entered World War 1 and sent troops to Europe under Pershing, US cavalry was little used, and in the period of change between the World Wars the cavalry regiments were mechanised. The horse, boots and saddle, and the sabre have gone – but the cavalry dash and spirit live on in the fast-striking armour and airborne troopers of the modern cavalry units.

7 · CAVALRY IN KHAKI

British cavalry galloped into the 20th century under fire from Boer sharpshooters during the South African War of 1899-1902. And with the regular army and yeomanry horsemen rode their colonial cousins from Australia, New Zealand, and Canada. Eighteen British cavalry regiments served in the Boer War but there was little opportunity for traditional shock tactics, the knee to knee charge in formation with sabre and lance. After a while the nature of the war and the unorthodox Boer adversary dictated that *l'arme blanche* give way to the rifle and carbine and the British cavalry increasingly played the role of mounted infantry.

The British had never met an enemy like the Boer, a guerrilla fighter *par excellence* armed with the latest weapons. The Boers, especially the back-veldt variety, were born to the saddle and the rifle. Natural horsemen and hunters, they became crackshots early in life. A father would give his son a

British cavalry column in South Africa during the Boer War.

British cavalry crossing a drift, or ford, under Boer gunfire. Illustration by John Charlton.

single bullet with which to shoot game for the day's pot; if the boy failed to hit his mark he went hungry. Masters of fieldcraft, the Boers fought from cover and when things started to go badly for them they would melt away. They saw no shame in flight; it enabled them to fight another day. They were prudent and practical horse soldiers. Not for them the crazy courage of the Zulu or Dervish who had charged *en masse* the British squares, only to be mowed down by disciplined firepower. The Boers did not fight to die, they fought to live, and they inflicted heavy losses on the British before bending the knee to a greater power.

The Boers (farmers) were the descendants of early Dutch and French Huguenot colonists in South Africa. When the Cape Colony passed into British control early in the 19th century the independent Boers, who disliked the British, trekked northward and established the republics of the Orange Free State and the Transvaal. When Britain annexed the troublesome Transvaal in 1877 the hostility between the Boers and the British led to the first Boer War of 1880-81. The redcoats suffered two humiliating defeats at Laing's Nek and Majuba Hill, an armistice was agreed and the Transvaal Boers won complete self-government. The discovery of diamonds and gold in the Transvaal brought in a flood of strangers. These uitlanders (foreigners) were soon at odds with the Boers.

218

Matters came to a head when the uitlanders plotted to overthrow the Transvaal government by force. The Boers crushed the uprising and the ensuing conflict of interests in South Africa sparked off the second Boer War between Britain and the allied Transvaal and Orange Free State.

The Boers were well armed with the German Mauser magazine rifle, machine guns and artillery. Every Boer male between 16 and 60 could be called upon to serve in a commando unit and at the outbreak of hostilities they were able to field some 40,000 men against the 10,000 British troops then in Africa. The war started badly for the British: they were soon besieged in Kimberley, Mafeking and Ladysmith and the first efforts to relieve these places ended in failure. In December 1899 came the stunning 'Black Week' in which the Boers inflicted disastrous defeats on the British at Stormberg, Magersfontein, and Colenso. In January 1900 came the Boer triumph at Spion Kop with much loss of British life, the latter disaster bringing about the replacement of the commander-in-chief Sir Redvers Buller with the old hero Lord Roberts.

In the beginning the British 'Tommy' clad in the modern khaki marched into battle in the old-fashioned drill book manner of close formations, with officers prominently leading and directing the action, the traditional style that had changed little from the Crimean War. The concealed, crackshot Boers would pick off the officers and, deprived of leadership, the soldiers were often thrown into disorder. British officers learned to be discreet in

'Goodbye Dolly Grey'. A Cavalryman leaves for South African service. The crown on his sleeve denotes that he is a Squadron Corporal Major of the Household Cavalry.

Lieutenant-Colonel G. H. C. Hamilton, commanding the 14th (King's) Hussars, uniformed and equipped for the Boer War. The regiment's badge – the crest of the Royal House of Prussia, seen here worn on the collar – was first adopted in 1798.

dress and in action, and the infantry came to use extended order, irregularity of line being required, regular dressing being avoided, and cover being taken when available. At first when the Colonial governments offered contingents to serve in South Africa, the British government asked only for infantry. But as the campaign progressed the 'top brass' realised the urgent need of more cavalry and horse soldiers. It was a war dominated by the magazine rifle and mounted infantry.

The new contingents were to consist entirely of mounted men and artillery. The first colonial troops to land in Cape Town were a detachment of New South Wales Lancers. About 90 of them had been in training in England at Aldershot with the 7th Dragoon Guards and when on their way

In stark contrast to the smartly turned out British cavalryman, a typical Boer horseman of the South African War.

Officer of the Victoria Mounted Rifles. Australians served with distinction in the Boer War.

home most of them volunteered to fight in South Africa. In all, Australia sent 16,632 officers and men to the Boer War, all the mounted men being excellent rough riders from the outback and sheep and cattle country. As scouts in a foreign land they were nearly as good as the Boers. The Australian Mounted Rifles and Mounted Infantry played a leading role in locating Piet Cronje and in recognition of this were given precedence over other troops when that skilful Boer general capitulated, and were first to enter the laager in which he had entrenched his men. Conan Doyle in *The Great Boer War*, 1901, said of the Australians:

'Amid all the scattered nations who came from the same home there is not one with a more fiery courage and higher sense of martial duty... than the men from the great island continent. It is the misfortune of the historian when dealing with these contingents that, as a rule, by their very nature they were employed in detached parties in fulfilling the duties which fall to the lot of scouts and light cavalry – duties which fill the casualty lists but not the pages of the chronicler. Be it said, however, once for all that throughout the whole African army there was

nothing but the utmost admiration for the dash and spirit of the hard-riding, straight-shooting sons of Australia and New Zealand. In a host which held many brave men there were none braver than they.'

One of Canada's most distinguished cavalry regiments, Lord Strathcona's Horse (Royal Canadians) was specially raised for service in the Boer War. The regiment took its name from its wealthy benefactor Donald A. Smith: Lord Strathcona and Mount Royal, who pledged to underwrite the raising and equipping of a new mounted regiment recruited from horsemen of the North West Territories. Smith, born in Scotland, entered the service of the Hudson's Bay Company and rose to become governor of the Company. In 1896 he was appointed Canadian High Commissioner to the British government and elevated to the peerage in the following year. He realised soon after the start of the Boer War the need for 'fighters of the type of Mounted Police of the Canadian prairies who would be more of a match for the Boers than the sedulously drilled infantrymen of the English pattern'.

Lord Strathcona proposed to raise, arm, equip and ship to South Africa at his own expense a mounted regiment of 400 (later increased to 540) men,

separate from the Canadian contingents already formed. The British government accepted the generous offer and Strathcona chose Superintendent Samuel B. Steele of the North West Mounted Police to command the regiment named Strathcona's Horse. Some 40 officers and men recruited were former 'Mounties.'

'The men enlisted,' Sam Steele said, 'are composed of the very pick of the cowboy, ranger, and policeman of the Territories and British Columbia. The balance are Westerners of varied experiences, especially qualified with rifle and horse... all of them used to long hours in the saddle, experienced men, very few under 25 and the majority over 30... well used to hard work, range riding, patrolling, surveying, prospecting, freighting and farming.'

While Steele recruited the men, Dr Duncan McEachern was out West buying suitable mounts for Strathcona's Horse. On 10 March 1900 he reported that he had purchased:

Sergeant Arthur Richardson of Strathcona's Horse won Canada's first VC in the Boer War.

'Sounding the Charge'. A cavalry trumpeter carried both a bugle for field calls and a trumpet for the more elaborate camp and barrack calls. Illustration by R. Caton Woodville.

225

'536 cow horses [nearly all of them] thoroughly broken to cowboy work – taught to rein by the neck, stop suddenly, turn on the hind feet as a pivot, stand with the reins over their heads on the prairie, ford and swim rivers, go at a rapid pace up or down hills. They are stout animals with good short backs and strong quarters, good bone and active as cats – horses which know nothing of stables or grooms, accustomed to be ridden half a day or more, and at night simply stripped of saddle and turned loose to find their food.'

These prairie ponies, unlike the well-bred English or Irish types of the British cavalry, were similar in toughness and endurance to the hardy

Basuto ponies ridden by the Boers, capable of covering some 50 miles a day on little grazing. Strathcona's Horse sailed from Halifax for the Cape on 16 March 1900 with 599 horses, of which 176 were lost *en route* from pneumonia. The survivors proved to be the best horses in service. 'At least a squadron of them,' said Sam Steele, 'lasted through the whole war and the remount officer at Macadorp stated that they were by far the best remounts he had seen.'

The Strathconas, attached to the 3rd Mounted Brigade commanded by Major General the Earl of Dundonald, had their baptism of fire on Dominion Day (the first day of July), 1900, when they suffered one man killed and two taken prisoner. The regiment's Sergeant Arthur H. Richardson, a former mounted policeman, was the first Canadian to win the Victoria Cross in the South African campaign. He – like most cavalry VCs in this war – earned his cross by saving a wounded comrade under heavy enemy fire.

'On July 5th, at Wolver Spruit, about 15 miles north of Standerton,' ran the official announcement, 'a party of Lord Strathcona's Corps, only 38 in number, came into contact and engaged at close quarters with a force of 80 of the enemy. When the order to retire had been given Sergeant Richardson rode back under a heavy crossfire and picked up a Trooper whose horse had been shot and who was wounded in two places and rode with him out of fire. At the time that this act of

In September 1901 at Blood River Poort some 500 Boer horsemen, shooting from the saddle, charged a strong column of guns and mounted infantry under Major Gough and annihilated the British force.

Here we see Corporal Long of the
17th Lancers at skirmishing drill in
1896. Four years later the regiment
saw hard service in the Boer War.

gallantry was performed Sergeant Richardson was within 30 yards of the enemy and was himself riding a wounded horse.'

After an arduous guerrilla campaign in pursuit of the scattered Boer forces in the latter stage of the war, Strathcona's Horse sailed for England in January 1901 and received a King's Colour from Edward VII. The regiment arrived in Canada in March and disbanded. In 1903 the Canadian Mounted Rifles were granted the prefix 'Royal' and in 1909 this regiment was renamed 'Lord Strathcona's Horse.' The addition of 'Royal Canadians' was authorised in 1911 to preserve the link with the Mounted Rifles, and Lord Strathcona's Horse (Royal Canadians) remains the regiment's official name.

Following the shock to the British nation of 'Black Week' in December

229

Strathcona's Horse, a Canadian regiment also specially raised for service in the Boer War. Note the regimental brand on the horse.

1899, all available reinforcements were sent out from the United Kingdom, including the crack 17th Lancers, the 'Death or Glory Boys', of whom more later. To ensure a supply of more mounted men the Imperial Yeomanry was created – recruited initially from the existing Yeomanry Cavalry regiments, and secondly from volunteers who could ride and shoot. Yeomanry units originated in the 18th century at the time of the Jacobite rebellion when local volunteer defence groups undertook to provide their own horses, uniforms and arms. The system was formalised in 1794 by Act of Parliament in defence of an England threatened with invasion by revolutionary France. The normal requirement of Yeomanry was the

A private in serge dress, 1900, Strathcona's Horse. Painted by R. Marrion.
Illustration supplied courtesy of Lord Strathcona's Horse (Royal Canadians).

defence of their own country. Some 10,000 Imperial Yeomanry went to South Africa between January and April 1900 and served as mounted infantry, equipped with Lee Metford rifle, bandolier and bush hat.

An early British victory in which cavalry played a prominent role took place at Elandslaagte on 21 October 1899. Major Wilcox of the 5th Royal Irish Lancers was there and describes the charge and pursuit:

'The Boers were streaming off their main position in a northerly direction, and with the 5th Lancer squadron on the right and the 5th Dragoon Guards on the left, the cavalry extended [in line formation] and were let go. As they topped the rise which

Kaiser Wilhelm II of Germany in the uniform of the Death's Head Hussars. When World War I broke out the Kaiser was also Colonel-in-Chief of Britain's 1st The Royal Dragoons.

had concealed them, they found the Boers crossing their front at a distance of a few hundred yards. For over a mile did the British squadron ride through the enemy, spearing some forty of them. Then rallying, the troopers wheeled about and galloped back again through the still streaming crowd of fugitives. Many Boers endeavoured to fire their Mausers from the saddle, but after the first onset of the cavalry, the Boers were straining every nerve to gallop away from those terrible lance points.'

The only cavalry *coup de main* of any distinction was that in which Sir John French, leading a cavalry division, sallied forth to relieve besieged Kimberley in February 1900. The division included a composite Household

German uhlans encountering barbed-wire defences outside Liège. Their uniform differs little from that worn in the Franco-Prussian War of 1870. Illustration by F. Matania and published in *The Sphere* of 15 August 1914.

Cavalry, the Scots Greys, the Inniskilling Dragoons, the 10th and 14th Hussars, the 9th, 12th and 16th Lancers, the New South Wales Lancers, the Carabineers, and seven batteries of the Royal Horse Artillery. Totalling 3,000 sabres, it was the largest mounted force fielded by the British army since Waterloo.

'The division is about to start on an expedition which it will remember all its life,' Lord Roberts told the men before marching out, 'and it rests with the division to show that it can maintain the traditions of the British cavalry and relieve Kimberley at all costs.'

The column started out at 2 am on 12 February. 'The long sinuous line of night-riders moved off over the shadowy veldt, the beat of twenty thousand hoofs, the clank of steel, and the rumble of gun-wheels and tumbrils swelling into a deep low roar like the surge upon the shingle.' Sir John French force-marched the division day and night until he came up against General Piet Cronje's army near the Modder River on the morning of 15 February. Conan Doyle describes the action:

'All That was Left of Them', a painting by R. Caton Woodville to commemorate the gallant stand of a squadron of the 17th Lancers when surrounded by Boers, as described in the main text.
Illustration supplied courtesy of The 17th/21st Lancers

Major-General J. M. Babington commanded the First Cavalry Brigade in South Africa during the Boer War.

Uhlan wearing drab cloth cover over his gleaming lancer cap for field service.

'Disregarding the Boer fire completely the cavalry swept in wave after wave over the low nek, and so round the base of the hills. The Boer riflemen upon the kopjes must have seen a magificent military spectacle as regiment after regiment, the 9th Lancers leading, all in very open order, swept across the plain at a gallop. A few score horses and half as many men were left behind them, but forty or fifty Boers were cut down in the pursuit... And now the [cavalry] had a straight run before it, for it had outpaced any further force of Boers which may have been advancing from the direction of Magersfontein. The horses, which had come a hundred miles in four days with insufficient food and water, were so done that it was no uncommon sight to see the trooper not only walking to ease his horse, but carrying part of his monstrous weight of saddle gear. But in spite of fatigue the force pressed on until in the afternoon a distant view was seen, across the reddish plain, of the brick houses and corrugated roofs of Kimberley. The Boer besiegers cleared off and

The Scots Greys, pictured here, landed in France on 17 August 1914 – 13 days after war had been declared – and moved up to the Belgian frontier as part of the 5th Cavalry Brigade. It became necessary to stain the famous grey horses a chestnut colour as camouflage and to prevent easy identification of their formation.
Illustration supplied courtesy of Lieutenant-Colonel R. B. Anderson

that night the relieving column camped on the plain two miles away, while French and his staff rode into the rescued city.'

The 17th Lancers arrived at Cape Town in March 1900, after a month at sea, and travelled by train to Bloemfontein, the recently captured capital of the Orange Free State. Here the 17th joined the Third Cavalry Brigade, which served as the flank guard of the army when it next advanced and took Pretoria, capital of the Transvaal. Although the British now occupied both capitals, Boer resistance was by no means crushed. After the dispersal of their main armies the Boers broke up into numerous small commandos: moving rapidly over great distances they attacked the long British lines of

237

Lord Roberts rides into Kimberley after the besieged city is relieved by Sir John French's cavalry division in February 1900.

communication between the Cape and Pretoria. In defence of these lines and to restrict the mobility of the raiders, Lord Kitchener (who had taken over from Lord Roberts) established a system of blockhouses, connected by barbed wire and manned by infantry, and used cavalry to sweep the areas in between.

The cavalry also endeavoured to surprise and destroy the commandos on the open veldt and the hard-riding 17th Lancers spent many months in these pursuits, On one occasion 'C' squadron was itself taken by surprise near Modderfontein Farm in the Tarkestadt District. The Boers, under Jan Smuts (who later became Prime Minister of South Africa), attacked at daybreak in a thick fog and opened fire at short range. Surrounded and outnumbered the 'Death or Glory Boys' fought back stubbornly, but with their ammunition exhausted and suffering heavy casualties their position

A British cavalry trooper and his mount in 1914, painted by Stanley L. Wood.

238

A photograph that points out the changing style of warfare. Aircraft and motor vehicles increasingly took over the traditional duties of cavalry, such as reconnaissance, patrol and communications.

was overrun. 'How gallantly those boys fought against us,' Smuts later wrote, 'many being killed because they knew not how to surrender.' In July 1901 the 17th Lancers got a new commanding officer in Colonel Douglas Haig, who 14 years later would be commander-in-chief of the British armies in France.

As the war progressed the growing force of British arms, and the relentless cavalry pursuit of the fragmented enemy, prevailed and the Boers finally conceded defeat. The war ended by the Treaty of Pretoria in May 1902. Writing on some military lessons learned from the war, Conan Doyle had this to say:

Belgian lancers in traditional
uniform pass through Charleroi in
1914.

'Passing on to the cavalry, we come to the branch of the service which appears to
me to be the most in need of reform. In fact the simplest and most effective reform
would be [to] abolish it altogether, retaining the household regiments for public
functions... Lances, swords, and revolvers have only one place – the museum.
How many times was the lance or the sword fleshed in this war, and how many
men did we lose in the attempts?... But if these various weapons are discarded
and we come down to the uniformity of the rifle, then of course we must teach the
trooper to use his rifle on foot and dress him so that he can do so. So in an
automatic and unavoidable way he becomes mounted infantry... Let a man be a
fine rider, a trained horsemaster, a good skirmisher, and a dead shot, and he
becomes more valuable than any mere cavalryman can be.'

Others, especially the hidebound cavalry establishment, did not agree
with Conan Doyle. Colonel Douglas Haig wrote in 1907 that 'the role of

241

Cavalry, far from having diminished, has increased in importance. It extends to both strategy and tactics; it alone is of use in the service of explorations and it is of capital importance in a general action.' And Colonal Robert Home, writing in 1903:

'The use of cavalry with skill at the right moment and in the right numbers has always been considered one of the most difficult problems in war; modern arms have increased this difficulty manifold, but to say that the day of cavalry on the field of battle is past, is merely an admission that the knowledge of how it should be used is wanting.'

In the static trench warfare of 1914-18 there was little use for mass cavalry action in the broken ground of the Western Front. Nevertheless large cavalry formations were held in reserve to exploit the great breakthrough that never materialised. The cavalry scouted, skirmished, ran messages, and fought dismounted as infantry. Reconnaissance could now be carried out by aircraft and balloons. It was apparent even in the earliest stages of the war that armoured cars were gradually displacing cavalry and that

Throughout the Great War, Britain's 21st Lancers (of Omdurman fame) served in India, fighting the hostile tribes of the North West Frontier. In September 1915 Private (Shoeing-smith) Charles Hull risked his own life to save Captain Learoyd, whose horse had been shot close to the enemy, by taking him up behind him and galloping to safety. Hull was awarded the Victoria Cross.

242

'The Charge of Flowerdew's Squadron' at Moreuil Wood in March 1918, an action in which the Canadian cavalry distinguished themselves. Painted by Sir Alfred Munnings.
Illustration supplied courtesy of the Canadian War Museum.

many duties hitherto carried out by horsemen were taken over by the faster motor car and motorcycle.

Although cavalry had little effect on the outcome of battles or campaigns in the European theatre there were many cavalry clashes and a number of do-or-die charges at infantry and guns. One in particular had strategic value – the action of the Canadian Cavalry Brigade at Moreuil Wood, northern France, on 30 March 1918. During their great March-April offensive the Germans were rapidly advancing on Amiens. Brigadier General Jack Seely, commanding the Canadian Cavalry Brigade, was ordered to cross the Avre river and engage the enemy ensconced on Moreuil Ridge and endeavour to delay him crossing the river. Seely rode ahead to scout the position. What he observed filled him with alarm:

'I saw at once that the position was desperate, if not fatal. If the enemy captured the ridge, the main line from Amiens to Paris would be definitely broken, and I already knew that when that happened the two armies – French and British – would be

243

compelled to retire; the French on Paris and our army on the Channel ports. All our sea power, even the great host of determined soldiers now crossing from the United States would not avail the Allied cause. All that we had fought for, and bled for, for nearly four years would be lost.'

General Silvestre (in forage cap) with French cavalry officers, who wear cloth covers over their crested cuirassier helmets.

Seely decided an immediate attack was essential before the Germans became firmly entrenched, and reinforced in Moreuil Wood on the ridge. He launched his Royal Canadian Dragoons and Lord Strathcona's Horse into action, holding the Fort Garry Horse in reserve. While dismounted troopers engaged the Germans in the wood, Lieutenant Gordon Flowerdew and his squadron of Strathconas rode to the east of the wood to catch the enemy coming out. There he ran into two lines of prepared German Grenadiers supported by machine-guns. Flowerdew had to make a quick cavalry decision. He could either retreat and suffer heavy losses in running away, or he could charge and suffer heavy casualties in trying to disperse the enemy.

Flowerdew turned in his saddle and shouted 'It's a charge, boys, it's a charge!' His trumpeter, riding behind him, was killed before he could blow the call. Despite frightful casualties the sabre-wielding Strathconas galloped through both lines of Germans, wheeled about and crashed through again, riding hell-for-leather for Moreuil Wood to join the other

A French cavalry versus German cavalry encounter early in the war, as depicted by F. Matania.

Canadians. Few survived. Flowerdew, mortally wounded, received a posthumous Victoria Cross. The Canadians, with reinforcements, secured the ridge. The German push of 30 March had been stopped dead at Moreuil Wood by cavalry action, albeit at great sacrifice. 'Your recapture of Moreuil Ridge was a great feat of arms,' General Rawlinson, commander of Fourth Army, told the survivors, 'it did much to turn the tide and save Amiens.'

Cavalry exercised a decisive influence in the successful British invasion of Palestine and Syria in 1917–18 directed by Major General Allenby. Edmund Allenby was a thoroughbred cavalryman, born in 1861 and commissioned into the Inniskilling Dragoons in 1882. He served in several African campaigns and distinguished himself as a column commander in the Boer War. He went on to command the 5th Royal Irish Lancers and the Fourth Cavalry Brigade. Between 1910 and 1914 he was Inspector-General of Cavalry. When war came in 1914 Allenby was given command of the Cavalry Division of the British Expeditionary Force sent to France, where he later commanded the Third Army.

In June 1917 Allenby was given command of the Egyptian Expeditionary Force which had ground to a halt, with heavy losses, in front of the Turkish positions defending Gaza. Allenby, a big, bluff and forbidding dragoon, known to his men as 'the Bull,' was exactly the right man to power one of the greatest campaigns in cavalry history. He was ordered to

break the deadlock and take Jerusalem before Christmas. His force amounted to some 80,000 men of whom 20,000 were mounted. It is interesting to note that no regular British cavalry took part in the campaign. Allenby's mounted arm comprised of British Yeomanry regiments (citizen-soldiers serving for the duration of the war) and light horse and mounted rifles of Australia and New Zealand. As in the Boer War the 'Anzacs' had answered the bugle call of the Motherland with alacrity and served with distinction.

'We say to you, Light Horsemen, whether fields are lost or gained,
Australia's pride is safe with you, you'll keep that pride unstained;
And though they praise the French Hussars, and Cossacks fierce and tall,
We know you'll prove on hard-held fields the equal of them all;
And when you ride with foamy reins, and spur-raked, heaving sides,
You'll show those German Uhlan chaps the way the Bushman rides.'

The difference between mounted infantry and light horse was that the first were foot soldiers provided with increased power of locomotion, whilst the second were horsemen trained to fight on foot in both offensive and defensive actions. The light horse were expected to perform the duties of

reconnoitring and screening troop movements as well as protecting from surprise attacks. The mounted infantry were picked soldiers often organised as small units as adjuncts to an infantry brigade, or to an independent force of cavalry.

Allenby's general plan of attack on the Turkish lines depended on taking the stronghold of Beersheba with its precious wells, and it was essential that it be captured quickly before its defenders could destroy the wells. The preparations for the attack on Beersheba were executed with the greatest secrecy, nearly everything being done at night. False reports and documents were carefully spread and mock preparations threatening Gaza were carried out openly. These moves persuaded the Turks that Gaza was the main objective and little was done to improve the Beersheba defences. After artillery had pounded the enemy lines at Gaza and sufficiently cut the wire entanglements, Allenby's infantry attacked.

Just after 4 pm on 31 October 1917 the 4th and 12th Australian Light Horse were ordered to charge the entrenched Turks defending Beersheba. Advancing at a trot and then at a gallop, the yelling Australians raced across the open country and dashed upon the enemy. Each trooper gripped his bayonet, sword fashion, his rifle being secured to the saddle. Fortunately for the charging horsemen, Turkish machine-guns had been silenced by the accurate shooting of the supporting field artillery battery. The light horsemen leaped the trenches, dismounted and jumped into the dugouts to tackle the Turks with their bayonets. Having cleared the trenches the horsemen galloped on into Beersheba. The swiftness and surprise of the assault proved successful: the town was occupied before the disorganised Turks had time to destroy the wells.

The first part of Allenby's plan had succeeded brilliantly. The Australian horsemen had taken some 1,500 prisoners and the city intact. Having captured Beersheba and then Gaza and driven the remnants of the defenders reeling northwards, it remained to keep the demoralised enemy on the run, to give him no time in which to reorganise, and to drive him through and beyond his next line of defences. And Allenby's horsemen pursued the enemy relentlessly in the best cavalry tradition. On one occasion Lieutenant Colonel Gray-Cheape and his Warwickshire Yeomanry were ordered to charge two batteries of guns supported by machine-guns which were protecting a Turkish rearguard. About 130 horsemen galloped into the face of withering fire; less than 60 reached the gunners, slashing left and right with their swords, killing most of the gunners at their posts and capturing twelve guns and three machine-guns.

Allenby's cavalry chased and punished the retreating enemy for some 20 miles. The retreat was saved from becoming a rout by the utter exhaustion of the pursuing horses and lack of water and provisions. Allenby's operations had broken the Turkish army into two separate parts, which retired north and east respectively. 'The Bull' barged on to Jaffa, the seaport of Jerusalem. At the Abu Shusheh ridge the British Yeomanry made another successful charge. Riding up a steep slope, heedless of heavy

General Sir Edmund Allenby. His brilliant and aggressive use of cavalry in Palestine and Syria brought about the defeat of Turkey.

machine-gun fire, the troopers stormed the ridge, sabring 400 of the enemy and capturing 360 men and a gun. There were many times during this campaign when cavalry in a spirited charge triumphed over infantry and machine-guns in position.

Allenby entered Jerusalem early in December 1917 and next planned his grand offensive against the Turkish-German forces in northern Palestine and Syria. Delayed by shortage of troops, he launched his new campaign on 19 September 1918. Allenby's army numbered some 60,000 men, of whom 12,000 were horsemen, and 540 guns. The enemy strength totalled about 40,000 men and 370 guns. It is interesting to note that the sword was issued to all ranks of the Australian Mounted Division prior to the general offensive. 'The issue of the sword was, I consider, more than justified,' said Brigadier General Wilson of the 3rd Australian Light Horse Brigade. 'I consider that the sword has a great moral effect both on the man carrying it and on the enemy. One of the chief values of the sword is the spirit of progress it inspires in the carrier.'

Allenby opened his attack with a shattering artillery barrage followed by a general advance. The guns of 21 Corps tore a wide gap on Allenby's left wing, through which raced the Desert Mounted Corps commanded by General Chauvel, an Australian cavalryman of distinction. The horsemen advanced upwards of 50 miles in 24 hours, and not without stiff fighting at several points. Allenby's left wing lay on the coast in the plain of Dothan.

249

The cavalry swung right through the Megiddo Passes and struck the enemy in the rear on the plain of Esdraelon, country admirably suited to the employment of cavalry.

Having traversed the Musmus pass during the night, the 4th Cavalry Division encountered a strong Turkish force near Megiddo on the plain of Esdraelon. The force had been sent almost a day earlier to occupy and defend the pass, but the swift-moving British cavalry had just got through in time. Advancing into the plain a regiment of Indian lancers, acting as vanguard, were confronted by an enemy battalion lightly dug in about two miles from the entrance of the pass. The lancers extended into line formation, sweeping forward at the trot, then broke into a gallop and crashed into the enemy ranks, killing 90, wounding many more and taking over 400 prisoners. Despite heavy fire the lancers never faltered, each wave riding through the Turks.

After this spectacular victory the column pressed on to El Affule railway junction and quickly captured it with its garrison of 1,500 men, 8 locomotives, 2 complete trains, 40 motor trucks, and huge quantity of stores. The main body of the division then marched up the valley of Jezreel to Beisan, occupying the railway and taking some 1,000 prisoners. Many of these cavalrymen had covered 70 miles in the two days, a remarkable feat in the circumstances. Other cavalry divisions entered Nazareth and further key objectives, cutting off the enemy and thrusting him against the river Jordan. Thus did Allenby's rapid advance, spearheaded by the Desert Mounted Corps, progress swiftly through northern Palestine and into Syria, reaching Aleppo on 25 October 1918.

In just over a month Allenby's forces, covering some 350 miles, had destroyed three Turkish armies and captured 75,000 prisoners, 360 guns and 800 machine-guns. A war-weary Turkey immediately sought peace and an armistice was signed on 30 October. British casualties amounted to 5,666 of whom 853 died. Allenby was made a field marshal and created a viscount, adopting the title Viscount Allenby of Megiddo and Felixstowe, thus acknowledging the brilliant breakthrough in the campaign that his biographer Field Marshal Earl Wavell called 'the most striking example of the power of the cavalry arm in the whole history of war.' Allenby, who died in 1936, was the last great captain of horse cavalry.

The end of the first world conflict sounded the final trumpet call for British cavalry in war. The advent of the tank and fast motor vehicles made mechanisation inevitable and by the outbreak of World War 2 most of the cavalry regiments of the major powers were mounted on the war horse of the 20th century: the armoured car and the battle tank. The cavalry spirit and tradition have, however, survived the transition, manifested in the dash and the duties required of the modern trooper.

BIBLIOGRAPHY

This is, of necessity, a select bibliography of primary and secondary references.

Bachrach, BS, 'Charles Martel, Mounted Shock Combat, The Stirrup and Feudalism', *Studies in Medieval and Renaissance History*, Vol. 8, Nebraska, 1970.

Brett-Smith, R, *The 11th Hussars*, London, 1969.

Childers, E, *War and the Arme Blanche*, London, 1910.

Conan Doyle, A, *The Great Boer War*, London, 1901.

Contamine, P, *War in the Middle Ages*, Oxford, 1984.

Dewing, HB (editor), *Procopius: History of the Gothic War*, London, 1911.

Duffy, C, *The Army of Frederick the Great*, London, 1974.

ffrench Blake, RLV, *The 17th/21st Lancers*, London, 1968.

Firth, CH, *Cromwell's Army*, London, 1902.

Fraser, WB, *Always a Strathcona*, Calgary, 1976.

Hatto, AT, 'Archery and Chivalry: A Noble Prejudice', *Modern Language Review*, Vol. 35, Cambridge, 1940.

Hennebert, E, *Nos Soldats*, Paris, 1888.

Keegan, J, *The Face of Battle*, London, 1976.

Lezius, M, *Das Ehrenkleid des Soldaten*, Berlin, 1936.

Longworth, P, *The Cossacks*, London, 1965.

Lunt, J, *Charge to Glory!*, London, 1961.

MacMunn, G, *The Armies of India*, London, 1911.

Marchant, EC (editor), *Xenophon: On the Cavalry Commander and On the Art of Horsemanship*, London, 1925.

Masson, F, *Cavaliers de Napoleon*, Paris, 1902.

Maude, FN, *Cavalry: Its Past and Future*, London, 1903.

Newark, TP, *The Barbarians*, Poole, 1985.

Nolan, LE, *Cavalry: Its History and Tactics*, London, 1853.

Preston, RMP, *The Desert Mounted Corps*, London, 1921.

Richard, W, *Her Majesty's Army*, London, 1891.

Rickey, D, *Forty Miles a Day on Beans and Hay*, Oklahoma, 1963.

Seaton, A, *The Horsemen of the Steppes*, London, 1985.

Urwin, JW, *The United States Cavalry*, Poole, 1983.

Vale, M, *War and Chivalry*, London, 1981.

Warner, P, *The British Cavalry*, London, 1984.

Wavell, AP, *The Palestine Campaign*, London, 1927.

White, L, *Medieval Technology and Social Change*, Oxford, 1962.

Wood, E, *Achievements of Cavalry*, London, 1897.

Woodham-Smith, C, *The Reason Why*, London, 1953.

Wormser, R, *The Yellowlegs: The Story of the US Cavalry*, New York, 1966.

PICTURE CREDITS

All pictures supplied courtesy of Peter Newark's Historical Pictures except for those on the following pages: 231, 234, 237, and 243.